A Wooddragon Book
www.wooddragonbooks.com

Published by: Martrain Corporate and Personal Development
Post Office Box 1216, Regina, Saskatchewan Canada
S4P 3B4
Telephone: 306.569.0388
www.martrain.org

Book and cover design by: Signature Graphics

First Edition: March 2013
ISBN: 978-0-9685370-3-9

GENERATION Y

and the NEW WORK ETHIC

Jeanne Martinson, M.A.

Early praise for

"Generation Y and the New Work Ethic"

"Jeanne Martinson's research and insights are invaluable to contemporary leaders navigating the challenges of managing across the generations. Whether you are an individual who is adjusting to having a boss younger than you, or you are a senior manager negotiating leadership across several generations, this book is pragmatic and instructive. Through the use of research analysis, common sense, and practical wisdom, Jeanne provides us with a roadmap for successfully navigating the difficult and challenging terrain of inter-generational leadership. This book is a "must read" for leaders looking to understand how to work creatively with different generations." - *Kathleen Thompson, PhD, Director - Canadian Mental Health Association (Saskatchewan Division)*

"OK...there are plenty of good books about age categories - the Gen X, Ys, etc. However, this book actually tells you what to do with all that information and how to effectively use it in your workplace. It is an easy read about a complex issue and an excellent dialogue opener for any manager, in any department, about organizational culture." - *Colleen Smith, Senior Executive*

"If you have ever complained about the 'young kids' in your workplace and their lack of a 'work ethic', I highly recommend Jeanne Martinson's new book. It's a simple and easy read that clearly explains why these 'young kids' are the way they are and why it is such a big deal for those of us who are simply young at heart. With the very specific instructions, Jeanne's book will become your everyday reference on how to manage a diverse workforce. I will be recommending it to all managers as well as my 21-year old Gen Y son who is currently learning to navigate the workplace."- *Carolyn Schur, Author of "Working 'Round the Clock"*

"As an employer I often feel that I just don't get it! Each employee reacts differently to situations. Now I know why!" - *Pat Dell, AMP, Broker Owner, Verico Crown Mortgage Services*

"Fascinating read and I can see this playing out in my workplace right now. Jeanne's keen observations and practical advice on inter-generational dynamics is a necessary read for any leader." - *Pamela Burns, Leadership Development Consultant*

"Good read and has given me some food for thought on how to deal with my staff. I have a better understanding as to why they make me feel like they aren't paying attention. It also solves some of my frustration level. I now have a way to sort out my workings." - *Nancy Bowey, Small Business Owner*

To Malcolm

Table of Contents

 # Introduction ———

Why is Generation Y So Different?

We have a perfect storm brewing for generational conflict in the workplace due to two unique factors:

First, we now have four distinct generational groups in the workplace. Thanks to interrupted plans for retirement due to the 2008 economic downturn, a genuine enjoyment of the work they are engaged in and an anticipation of a longer life span, members of our oldest generation find themselves still in the workplace. At the same time, the Baby Boomers are mid-career to closing in on retirement and are primarily occupying the positions of power in our organizations. Due to advanced health care providing expectations of a long and healthy life, and meaningful work to occupy themselves with, Baby Boomers may be finding the workplace more attractive and will possibly push back retirement plans. Gen Xs, in their early 30s to late 40s are waiting impatiently for better career

opportunities to materialize, while Generation Y is close on Generation X's heels, bursting into the workforce with their enthusiasm and expectations of a brave new world.

Secondly, Gen Ys came into the workforce at the end of the analog to digital shift. This is highly significant as Gen Ys are the first generation to see digital technology as normal, both in their work and personal life.

These two factors have collided to place employees from different generations in heightened conflict with each other. In the workplace, these different generations are now judging each other as having good or poor work ethic, commitment and loyalty to the organization.

A '**perfect storm**' is a term used to describe a rare combination of circumstances that leads to an aggravated situation or an event of unusual magnitude. Awareness of this perfect storm of generational conflict has driven me to delve deeper into the circumstances at its cause such as work ethic and attitude. The result of my efforts has been this book. I sincerely hope this research will help you better understand this workplace weather system.

Chapter One
Defining the Generations

The term **generation** derives from Latin and means "to beget". In kinship, familial or biological terminology, it is a structural term designating the parent-child relationship. **Generation,** however, has also come to be used to describe a cultural subgroup or cohort within social science. It is important, therefore, to distinguish between familial and cultural generations.

A **familial generation** is often seen as the average time between a mother's first offspring and her daughter's first offspring. In Canada, for example, the average age of a first-time mother in 1983 was 26.9 years of age. In 2012, 29 years later, the average first-time mother was well over 29 years old. Similarly, as of 2008, the average generation length in the United States was 25 years, up 3.6 years from 1970. Germany saw a large increase in generation length over that time period, from 24 years in 1970 to 30 years in 2008.

So a generation, in context to family or human biology, is a span of approximately 29-30 years.

Social generations are cohorts of people who share similar cultural experiences and who were most likely born in the same date range. The idea of a cultural generation, in the sense that it is used today, was first coined in the late 19th century and by the beginning of the 20th century, the rebellion and emancipation of youth gave light to the idea that a group of younger people who experience the same social issues may be in themselves a type of 'generation'.

Two factors influenced the acceptance of this idea. First, young men were less likely to be financially dependent on their fathers, and secondly, they were less likely to follow in their father's vocational footsteps. Economic and social mobility allowed them to rebel to a greater degree than generations before. This younger generation also perceived that the skills and knowledge of their father's generation were not necessary significantly useful to them due to increases in technology.

Author Auguste Comte in his *Cours de philosophie positive,* explored the conflict arising between an aging generation and the rebellion of the following one, suggesting that as the members of a given generation age, their "instinct of social conservation" increases and brings them into conflict with the attitudes of the next, younger generation.

Karl Mannheim, in his 1923 essay, *The Problem of Generations,* suggested that there was more to this generational stuff, that it was not enough to just study generations as Comte did, measuring social change in fifteen to thirty year life spans. Mannheim said this reduced history to a mere chronological table, and that

qualitative experiences of the individual needed to be taken into consideration.

Since Comte and Mannheim's time, other academics, researchers and authors have attempted to make sense of the social generational phenomena, identifying generational year bands and characteristics of each generation and the impact on current society and work.

When Does a Generation Begin and End?

The span of when exactly a generation starts and ends differs from researcher to researcher.

The **Traditionalist** generation were born starting in the early to mid-1920s and ended in 1942 (N. Howe and W. Strauss), in 1946 (D. K. Foot), or in 1945 (D. Tapscott). This generation is sometimes also called the **silent** generation. Their childhoods and early adulthoods were defined by conflict and strife, notably the depression era of the 1930s and World War Two.

Baby Boomers were born between 1943 and 1960 (N. Howe and W. Strauss), between 1943 and 1960 (R. Zemke), between 1947and 1966 (D. K. Foot), or between 1946 and 1964 (D. Tapscott). This generation following World War Two was marked by a large increase in birth rates. In Canada, many Baby Boomers lack childhood recollection of war.

The generation following the Baby Boomers identified as **Generation X** were born between 1961 and 1981 (N. Howe and W. Strauss), between 1965 and 1975 (D. Tapscott), or between 1960 and 1980 (R. Zemke). This generation was smaller than the Baby Boomer generation it followed and smaller in Canada than Generation Y that they preceded.

Generation Y were born between 1982 and 2005 (N. Howe and W. Strauss), between 1977 and 1997 (D. Tapscott), between 1978 and 1990 (B. Tulgan), or born between 1980 and 2000 (R. Zemke). This generation can sometimes also be called Millennials, the iGeneration, Generation@, or Net Generation. They are the generation of children from small families. This book focuses on those Gen Ys who are currently or are about to join the workforce.

We Don't All Belong

We cannot assume that generational information applies across all cultures and geography. For example, in China, the Generation Y generation are optimistic for the future, have excitement for entrepreneurship and consumerism. They embrace the idea that they will be the generation to create the economic superpower of modern China. The Generation Y of Hong Kong, however are seen to be post-materialist in outlook, and they are vocal on anti-colonialism, sustainable development, and democracy.

Generational information is only one area of diversity that determines our beliefs and behaviours. Humans are like onions, with many layers. Some layers are more influential on our worldview than others. For example, even if a person falls in the Generation Y age band, if they are a new Canadian coming from a country where they felt economic or physical threat, they may respond to the world more like a Traditionalist.

We will discuss this idea further in Chapter Seven.

Can I be in Two or Have My Own? Jonesers and Zoomers

People born in generational cusp years demonstrate behaviors of the two groups they are closest to. For example, someone born in 1962 and probably technically a Baby Boomer could have both Baby Boomer and Generation X behaviors and beliefs. One generational group flows into the next. In this way, we understand how those born in cusp years (a handful of years on each side of a demographic boundary) behave like a hybrid of the two groups they are sandwiched between.

However, author Jonathan Pontell, who is receiving credit for tagging the latter decade of the Baby Boomer generation with the name **Generation Jones**, suggests that there is more to this decade of late Boomers than just the crossover effect of being born in the first or last years of a demographic era. He suggests that **Jonesers** are different enough from both Gen Xs and Baby Boomers to justify their own generational tag.

Pontell surveyed 1200 Americans born between 1954 and 1965, the younger decade of the Boomer generation. He found that less than 10% felt like either a Boomer or a Gen X. More than 80% said that they felt in-between the generations. Although that seems to reinforce the cusper theory, Pontell thought that it meant this decade is somehow special.

In the United States, Jonesers were too young to be engaged in the anti-war movement, political activism, fashion changes, music redirection and the Woodstock thrills that dominated the youth of the first decade of Baby Boomers. As well, they have been excluded from the political and economic agenda of America which has been dominated by the older Baby Boomers. Although the world is telling Baby Boomers as a whole that they are the generation in control of the system, Jonesers feel that not only are they *not* in the driver's seat, but have been tossed in the trunk along with the luggage and are merely along for the ride.

In their late 40s to late 50s today, Jonesers continue to feel second class to the power of the older Baby Boomers who are now approaching retirement and shifting the political and social agenda to reflect their changing needs. The older Boomer's outlook is significantly different from the younger Jonesers who are now in their prime earning years.

Most Jonesers are at a place where older Baby Boomers were a decade earlier – children, cars, homes, and retirement savings plans. Yet they resist being termed a Baby Boomer and don't want to be identified with that group. Some of this resistance is the residue of being left behind when the economic and political bus left town, but Pontell thinks it is more than that. Jonesers often want to distance themselves from the Baby Boomer identity because they believe Boomers talked about social conscience but eventually aligned themselves with the existing corporate and government systems. Boomers began fighting the establishment but ended up being the establishment. That is not who Jonesers are! They want real action, true practical change, and significant political discussion.

So is a Joneser just a Boomer with a social conscience or a Gen Xer with childcare issues and a mortgage? Or do they really see the world differently? Whether you believe Generation Jones is a subset of Baby Boomers or merely proves the cuspers theory, organizations need to be aware of the dangers of pigeonholing any person too tightly regarding one aspect of their diversity. A retiring Baby Boomer will be different than a Boomer who is 50 because generational grouping is only one of many ways we are different from each other. Information about any group gives us insight to assist us in effectively marketing to and motivating that group. The danger lies in assuming that someone from a certain group will behave according to the beliefs we have about that group.

Zoomers is a term that has also been tossed around in marketing and human resource literature, but unlike Jonesers, does not have any firm research grounding it in its argument for specialness. It is sometimes used to describe zippy Boomers, those older Boomers with a young heart and loads of energy. It has also been used to describe the chronologically younger decade of the Baby Boomer generation. Regardless of its journey into our vocabulary, it is a marketing term and not a social generational definition.

In the next four chapters, we will discuss the four unique generational groups at play in the workplace.

Chapter Two

The New Work Ethic

Over the past several years of presenting workshops on diversity issues and generational differences, one of the ideas that has continued to surface is Baby Boomers' and Gen Xs' perception that Gen Ys have little or no **work ethic.**

In researching this book, I sent out a request to my contacts through social media as well as posted notices to several on-line bulletin boards. The question I posed was: "Does Generation Y (ages 18-32 or so in the workplace) have a different work ethic than Baby Boomers? How specifically? What has been your experience?"

I was not surprised to have received several hundred replies. The responses included short quips, detailed personal experiences, warnings and rants. Although a handful replied that "No, they didn't see a difference in work ethic", the majority weighed in on the other side of the question and then gave me examples supporting their point.

When I asked the responders to define work ethic, they were stumped. They gave me further examples of behaviours that demonstrated what they believed to be good or poor work ethic, but defining the term 'work ethic' itself challenged them. When I pushed for a definition, I received answers such as: caring about your job, being respectful to others, being honest, being accountable, reliable and responsible.

How do we measure whether we or others have a good work ethic or a bad one if we can't even define the term?

The fact that we use the words **good** and **bad** is a clue that this issue is heavily laden with value interpretations. We seem to define work ethic as a laundry list of value interpretations. But who is defining the interpretations of those values and do we have mutual agreement? Some individuals I surveyed suggested that we don't have to define **work ethic**, that understanding what is a good work ethic is just common sense. However, is there really a common sense – a mutual agreement of specific behaviour that we can define as good or bad?

I turned to Joseph Sherren to gain clarity on this topic. Sherren teaches the *Principles of Ethics* at York University's Schulich School of Business in Canada, and works with organizations around the world as a consultant concerning this issue. Sherren insists that the term **work ethic** itself is a misnomer and that is why it is so difficult to define. "Ethics are a code of behavior acceptable to a group or organization. Not all organizations or groups uphold the same ethics. To suggest that someone is **unethical** can only be determined if the person's behavior is outside of the agreed upon ethics of the group to which that person belongs."

The challenge, of course, is that often groups do not discuss, let alone agree upon ways of behaving. This opens the door for us to judge another person's behavior negatively simply because the other person does not behave as we would.

Our personal ethics are often our espoused values. When an individual lives with integrity or behaves in alignment with their ethics, they are congruent and therefore considered ethical. Our scruples (or conscience) is the restraining force that keeps us in alignment (or in integrity) with our values. Our scruples are shaped by the negative and positive consequences we experienced as a result of our past behavior.

Sherren argues, if as a child we stole a chocolate bar and were caught and severely disciplined, we would have developed strong scruples in relation to shoplifting. However, if we stole a chocolate bar in our youth and were not caught, or were caught and not disciplined, our scruples in this area would be weaker. We may also be more inclined to see stealing in the future as more acceptable. Internally, we will experience guilt when we are not living in alignment with our values or personal ethics.

Most people see themselves as responsible, honest, innovative, reliable and accountable. However, often in the workplace, our morals (or personal interpretation of the stated values) are not always in agreement with everyone else's. This is where conflict arises and therefore the need for organizations and groups to clearly articulate ethical guidelines (also known as codes of behavior or codes of conduct).

The ethics of our work have to be defined, verbalized and documented. Those ethics (documented as a code of ethics, code of behaviour, or code of conduct) have to be clearly communicated. Consequence, both positive and negative, must follow adherence and lack of adherence to this code.

A Code of Ethics could focus on a particular area of concern. For example, a past client of MARTRAIN, my consulting firm, was struggling with the conflicting explanations for good and poor work ethic on his team regarding respectful behaviour between colleagues. We reduced the individual team members' definitions of work ethic down to individual behaviours that the client group wanted to encourage (good work ethic) and discourage (poor work ethic) on their team. From this, we crafted a **respect charter** which everyone signed and to which each team member became accountable. The client group, in fact, created what they would define as their idea work ethic.

Although we use the term **work ethic**, most people are referring to the relationship they have with the work itself and with others involved in their work. We may not be able to eradicate the term **work ethic** from our vocabulary, but we can begin to define and understand it to minimize generational conflict.

The New 'Work Ethic'

Consider six key areas where we have expectations of ourselves and others in the workplace:

1. Education
2. Experience
3. Enthusiasm and Energy
4. Endurance and Effort
5. Eloquence
6. Etiquette

By unbundling work ethic into these six areas, we can explain our expectations of others and communicate what we bring to the table. By clearly defining these areas in our work teams or organizations, we can move toward effective performance management as a leader (see Chapter Eight for more on this idea), minimize intergenerational conflict (see Chapter Seven for more on this), or increase our visibility and promotability as a Generation Y member (see Chapter Nine for more on this idea).

How would you score yourself on the new work ethic?

1. Education. Do you reach out to learn in formal and informal ways so as to be able to deliver higher value to your employer? Do you search out and embrace opportunities to learn from others and be mentored? Do you seek out knowledge outside of learning opportunities designated by your manager?

2. Experience. Do you search out opportunities to try new tasks and take on new responsibilities? Can you transfer these experiences into wisdom that can be used in similar or dissimilar situations? Can you successfully mentor others with your wisdom?

3. Enthusiasm and Energy. Do you come to work each day with a positive attitude? Do you manage your physical health so you have the energy to do the required tasks with acceptable speed and accuracy?

4. Endurance and Effort. Are you willing to continue on task to completion? Do you push through difficult or complicated tasks to completion? Do you continue with new tasks until you develop new knowledge or skills? Do you have the patience to complete mundane tasks that you may consider not a good match for your skill and knowledge level?

5. Eloquence. Can you communicate persuasively in written, verbal and person-to-person formats? Can you work with individuals different than yourself effectively?

6. Etiquette. Do you know at what levels of an organization an issue should be addressed? Can you successfully determine which format of communication (text, email, letter, over the phone or in person) is required for the level of complexity and conflict in the communication?

As we explore the four generational groups in the next chapters, notice which generations are more or less successful in each of the work ethic key areas.

Chapter Three

The Loyal Traditionalists

Many people wonder why, if Baby Boomers are starting to retire, do we continue to discuss the impact of Traditionalists in the workplace? There are several reasons for this:

One reason is the cusp effect. As mentioned earlier, cusp years are the handful of years at the beginning or end of a generation. Traditionalists cusping down to Baby Boomers are in their late to mid-60s today. Baby Boomers cusping up to Traditionalists are in their late 50s to mid-60s. Both of these cusp groups may identify with Traditionalists' history, motivations and attitudes.

Secondly, in small and particularly family owned businesses, senior members of the organization can easily be in their 60s, 70s or even 80s. Understanding this group as a colleague, employee, leader, customer and supplier is important.

Thirdly, current members of boards of directors of for-profit and non-profit organizations lean towards the Baby Boomer and Traditionalist generations.

Lastly, since the 2008 financial crisis, older Canadians simply do not have the financial resources to retire. Francis Fong, an economist with TD Economics states that "inadequate savings from earlier on in life has led many to work in retirement to supplement their income. In no small part, this would have been exacerbated by the decline in retirement assets in the wake of the 2008 financial crisis." The idea of 'Freedom 55' which was a marketing mantra in the past for early retirement has been exchanged for 'Security 66' as a new retirement goal.

We will likely find ourselves discussing the Traditionalist generation for a while yet. But, ten years from now, with another decade of aging upon us all, the Traditionalist generation will affect us less as its members will by then have moved through and out of the workplace.

The Childhood of the Traditionalist

The Traditionalist generation came of age during the depression era, surrounded by crisis, concern, instability and family loss. This formed a unique perspective in how they saw the world and the workplace.

In Canada, many non-Aboriginal Traditionalists were only one or two generations from immigration and as a result brought the immigrant perspective to their work. They also entered the workforce before benefits such as sick leave, stress leave, maternity leave, legislated workplace safety policies, and in some cases, paid holidays existed.

These realities created an employee loyal to the organization to an extreme degree, often willing to do work that was mundane, dirty, or unsafe. For early Traditionalists particularly, this was just how employment was and they had no significant expectations of engaging, meaningful work with happy, friendly others that later generations would demand.

During the 1980s, I had several jobs while I found my niche in life. Each time I left a job, I had a new and more exciting one in the offer. On the day of one such change, I called my father, confident that he would be as excited as I with the new path I had chosen.

The conversation went like this:

First call
Jeanne: *Dad, guess what?*
Dad: *Oh no, you quit another job!*
Jeanne: *Yes, but let me tell you about the new ...*
Dial tone (Dad had hung up on me)

Second call
Jeanne: *Dad! Wait! Let me tell you ...*
Dad: *What was wrong with your last job?*
Jeanne: *I wasn't learning anything new.*
Dad: *Who says you are supposed to learn at work, you are there to do a job.*
Jeanne: *And I wasn't having any fun.*
Dad: *Who says work should be fun?*
Jeanne: *And I wasn't making any interesting friends.*
Dad: *Who says you should be friends with those you work with?*

The telephone call occurred in 1986 and I only began to reflect on the significance of it twenty years later. My father, a Traditionalist on the oldest edge of the generation, saw work as somewhere you went, completed your day to the best of your ability and then went home to a life unrelated to your job.

The personal life of this generation, consisting of family, friends, volunteer service and spirituality, was separate from their work life. There were no work life balance concerns for Traditionalists. They were either at work or not at work. They existed in two separate worlds. Unless they were an entrepreneur, business owner or a professional in the medical field, when the work day was done - it was done.

Their friends were often from their neighbourhood, religious community, or service clubs. Their volunteer efforts were spent with their service clubs and religious organizations. According to Sarah Sladek, author of *The End of Membership as We Know It*, it was under the leadership of this generational group and older Baby Boomers, that many service clubs and member associations thrived as they didn't before and haven't since. The spiritual paths of Traditionalists were shared within their family and religious communities, but were rarely discussed or shared with their workmates.

This is a vastly different picture than the one we see today in most workplaces, where teammates socialize together, raise charity dollars through workplaces schemes, and discuss religious ideas openly and encourage others to share theirs.

Employer-Employee Agreement

Through most of the Traditionalists' work lives, there existed an unwritten but nonetheless fully understood agreement that if an employee worked hard and gave the organization their all, the organization would employ, reward and promote them appropriately. This philosophy created rules that everyone understood and followed. An employee rarely questioned directives of their leader. In fact, the word **leader** was rarely used. Organizational structure was stiff and concrete, and everyone knew who was where in the system.

Leaders were directive and authoritarian. They were often addressed formally by their subordinates and direct reports. The relationship between supervisor and employee was friendly, but neither expected to be each other's friend. Employees knew that their next step on the ladder to success was determined by their immediate supervisor and they respected that, even if they thought that person was incompetent.

No News Is Good News

In 1983, after moving to the United States, I found a job in industrial public relations. A few months in, I felt I was doing a good job, but was receiving no feedback, negatively or positively, from my manager. I went into his office, closed the door and confronted him. *"I need to know,"* I said, *"how am I doing here?"* He replied, *"You're not fired, are you?"* That was a Traditionalist's idea of feedback. The **no news is good news** way of managing subordinates. Each generational group has widened, deepened and formalized the expectations and processes of feedback, an outcome that puzzles some Traditionalists.

The 20 Year Old Traditionalist

Interestingly, there is one form of Traditionalist that does not fit the classic definition. Traditionalist characteristics (do what the manager requests even if you don't agree, put up with difficult work arrangements and bad leadership, wait for your opportunities) are rooted in a youth coloured by crisis and change. Similarly, a new immigrant coming to Canada from a nation in unrest, who has experienced economic or physical threat, will behave like a Traditionalist regardless of their chronological age.

This new Traditionalist may be willing to accept jobs some Canadians refuse to do and to live in accommodations that seem overcrowded and uncomfortable to a middle-class Canadian.

The Traditionalist, whether over 60 or under 30, focuses on being a loyal, dedicated, compliant and diligent employee. They want to be part of an organization's legacy and success. If they believe the organization is stable and will maintain the employer-employee agreement, they will stay long term with an organization and wait for their chance for promotion.

⚭ Chapter Four ———

The Busy Baby Boomers

Economic hardships of the depression era resulted in significant numbers of people delaying marriage and delaying having children. Most industrialized nations, including Canada, saw birth rates drop. With the economy picking up and more men in the marriage pool following the end of World War Two, optimism and opportunity led to a boost in the baby business. The result was the largest social and biological generation in Canadian history – the Baby Boomer generation. From 253,000 births in Canada in 1940 to a high in 1960 of 479,000, the birth surge was dramatic.

Many books have been written describing the influence of this generation, the largest in history. The Boomer generation changed our society starting from their first breaths, as we saw an increase in every service and product they needed or desired. David K. Foot in his book *Boom Bust and Echo* describes this effect, using examples ranging from primary schools to tennis courts.

Unlike the previous generation, Boomers lack any childhood recollection of World War Two except through the memories shared from family. Canada itself was not at war during the time of age of the development of the Baby Boomers, but early Boomers were impacted by the Korean War of 1950 to 1953 and later Boomers were impacted by the October Crisis of 1970.

The Korean War began in 1950 and Canada became involved as part of the British Commonwealth Forces Korea in 1951. The **British Commonwealth Forces Korea** was the formal name of the Commonwealth army, naval and air units serving with the United Nations (UN) in the Korean War and included forces from Australia, Britain, Canada, India and New Zealand. Canada sent 26,791 troops to fight in Korea and sustained 1,558 Canadian injuries and 516 deaths. Although often overshadowed by the Canadian contributions in the two world wars, the Korean War impacted the early Boomers and their perspective of the world.

The October Crisis was a series of events triggered by two kidnappings of government officials by members of the FLQ (*Front de libération du Québec*) in October 1970 in Quebec. This crisis led to the only peacetime use of the War Measures Act in Canada's history, occurring simultaneously with the deployment of Canadian Forces troops in Ottawa and Quebec, and the arrest by police of 497 people.

From 1963 to 1970 the Quebec nationalist group, the FLQ, detonated over 95 bombs with the largest single bombing being at the Montreal Stock Exchange on February 13, 1969, resulting in injury to 27 people. By 1970, 23 members of the FLQ were in prison.

On October 5th, the FLQ kidnapped the British Trade Commissioner James Cross from his home with a demand for the exchange of Cross for a number of convicted or detained FLQ members and a broadcast of their manifesto.

October 10th, the FLQ kidnaped the Minister of Labour for Quebec, Pierre Laporte.

The following day, the Canadian Army was sent to patrol the Ottawa region. On October 16th, Quebec Premier Bourassa requested that the government of Canada grant the government of Quebec emergency powers to allow them to apprehend and keep in custody individuals. This resulted in the implementation of the War Measures Act, allowing the suspension of *habeas corpus*, giving wide-reaching powers of arrest to police.

On October 17th, the FLQ announced that hostage Pierre Laporte had been executed.

As for James Cross - the FLQ reported that he would not be released until their demands were met which included the publication of the FLQ manifesto, the release of 23 political prisoners and an airplane to take them to either Cuba or Algeria.

On December 3rd in Montreal, after being held hostage for 62 days, kidnapped British Trade Commissioner James Cross was released after negotiations with police. Simultaneously, the five known kidnappers, Marc Carbonneau, Yves Langlois, Jacques Lanctôt, Jacques Cossette-Trudel and his wife, Louise Lanctôt, were granted safe passage to Cuba by the government of Canada after approval by Fidel Castro. On December 23rd, Prime Minister Pierre Trudeau announced that all troops

stationed in Quebec would be withdrawn by January 5th, 1971. On December 28th, the three members still at large (Paul Rose, Jacques Rose, and Francis Simard) were arrested and later charged with the kidnapping and murder of Pierre Laporte.

The events of October 1970 galvanized support against violence related to efforts for Quebec sovereignty and highlighted the movement towards political means of attaining greater autonomy and independence, including support for the sovereigntist *Parti Québécois*, which went on to form the provincial government of Quebec in 1976.

Although rarely discussed today, the PLQ crisis shaped mid to late Baby Boomers' perspective of Canada as a country where civil unrest, even separation was a possibility.

The Benefits of Following the Traditionalists

The earliest Baby Boomers were born into the prosperous post-war era when work was easy to find, a stark comparison to the Traditionalist generation before them and to the Generation X that followed.

Mass communication shifted from the radio of the Traditionalists era to the television of the Boomer generation as technology evolved. The slide-rule stepped aside for the adding machine in the workplace and the calculator in school. Workplace expectations increased in terms of what a person could achieve, own and be.

Boomers benefited from the hard work and sacrifices of the generation before and expected to achieve what Traditionalists had achieved and then some. Now more

accessible and affordable, post-secondary education was seen as a reasonable and achievable goal for most Baby Boomers, whether they gained it immediately after high school, part time through their working years or during a sabbatical time off.

Baby Boomers at Work

Baby Boomers desired a more democratic, flat organizational structure with greater control over their work life. This democratic perspective was reflected in Boomers' willingness to slightly bend the rules which Traditionalists had followed blindly, and encouragement of informal and friendly relationships with superiors and subordinates alike.

Traditionalists were loyal to the organization itself but Boomers bonded with their colleagues and their loyalty was focused on their team or department, versus the company at large. As Baby Boomers entered the workplace, there was also a shift to business strategies where budgets and goals were departmentally controlled and this further enforced the Boomer's desire to dedicate their loyalty to their group versus the organization as a whole.

A Boomer's self-worth is often tied to what he or she does for a living and their role within the workplace. As this generation began to take on responsibilities in the workplace, their connection to their role resulted in business cards describing all types of positions, not necessarily just ones in sales and marketing or the executive office.

It is a common saying that Baby Boomers 'live to work and other generations work to live'. This looks like it is

true on the surface, but it is more valid to say that "Boomers life is at work." Traditionalists separated their personal life from their business life, but Baby Boomers are friends with workmates, volunteer with workmates and even vacation with workmates. This is the generation that introduced the idea of workplace volunteering and paved the way for the United Way Thermometer poster. Older Traditionalists who were inclined to keep personal matters outside of the workplace, now reluctantly found themselves raising money for humanitarian causes side by side with their manager and administrative assistant.

The Medal of Busy

Baby Boomers created a value system in the workplace around the concept of busy. Often looking at activity and how something is done is seen as a priority over getting the task completed. Working long hours and traveling long distances are seen as medals of honour in the battle to build a career for Boomers.

Boomers are the most likely of the four groups to take work on holiday, remain connected to work while on holiday and take fewer of the holiday weeks than they have accrued. This is particularly obvious in Canada versus the USA. In the United States, paid holidays are more difficult to accrue and are therefore more likely to be used. Also in the USA, women do not have federally regulated maternity leave, so many people book their paid vacation days to provide care to their newborn child or grandchild. In Europe, not taking a certain number of your paid holiday days is seen by many employers as a negative action. European employers feel that employees need to be rested to be effective and creative.

The balance between process and progress has been different with each generational group. Traditionalists put progress over process, Baby Boomers place process over progress. Baby Boomers are often seen by the other three generations as wasting time with socializing in the workplace instead of getting down to the business at hand.

The Job Security Myth

Traditionalists entered the workplace during the time of the employer-employee relationship where the employer employed the employee and the employee gave his or her best to the organization. Traditionalists were raised in a time of turbulence and had low expectations of job security or tenure so even when they enjoyed a long job history with one organization, they were cautious about counting that it would go on indefinitely.

To a Traditionalist, a loss of employment meant that the organization had ceased to exist, downsized or the employee had done something extremely wrong and was let go. Traditionalists valued steady work and rarely left organizations voluntarily. They worked hard and hoped to be noticed.

The Baby Boomers are the first and last generation to both expect and receive job security. Where Traditionalists did not take for granted the employment they had, Boomers were raised in a time of optimism, economic growth and expansion. They had seen a man land on the moon. Anything was possible.

Once in the workplace, this desire for longevity defined their career strategy. Baby Boomers attempted to align themselves with those who could assist their career aspirations. This political bent was reflected in the discretionary distribution of information, learning who could help or mentor them to the next step up the ladder.

This plan for long term employment with one organization was hit hard by the economic downturn that followed the tech-bubble collapse and the events of 9-11 and Baby Boomers who were let go were more likely to be resentful and bitter than Traditionalists who were downsized. Baby Boomers had expectations that were not fulfilled and therefore had high levels of disappointment. They felt they had a right to their positions – hadn't they worked hard and done all the right things to ensure they were secure?

Baby Boomers are Very Diverse

With the oldest Boomers approaching retirement age, younger members of the generation are still in their late forties, and many have yet to leave their mark upon history and still have time in which to do so. Consider the diversity of those who fall under the generational Boomer title: Bobby Orr, the hockey player (born in 1948), Steve Jobs, the founder of Apple Computer (1950), cellist Yo-Yo Ma (1950), Tom Hanks, the actor (1956), Michael J. Fox (1961), Wayne Gretzky (1961), Jim Carrey (1962), and Mike Myers (1963).

There is no doubt a difference between how Bobby Orr and Mike Myers see the world, as they bookend the time band for Baby Boomer births. Both were considered to be born in cusping or crossover years (the last few years of one generation or the first few of the next). If you were

born in the last few or first few years of a generation, ask yourself whether you feel you are firmly in one generation or the other. Or do you feel you have one foot in the earlier generation and one foot in the following generation?

How Baby Boomers See Themselves

In corporate workshops I have conducted over the past several years, I have asked Boomers, Gen Xs and Gen Ys to explain to the other generations in the room what people need to know about them, what their challenges and fears are and what others can do to help them feel respected in the job.

Here are some of their reflections:

Baby Boomers want others to know that although they have been around for a while they do know what they are talking about. Reward, recognition, and acknowledgement are important (especially from younger generations). They bring significant experience and knowledge to the task and life experience counts for something.

Baby Boomers feel that they are now challenged by technology (they can learn it but it takes more time and practise and it takes enormous effort just to keep up), the speed of change, having to adopt ideas that are not their own, balancing work life and the needs of aging parents, the natural aging process, understanding and working with other generations, the temptation to take work home or stay late when others don't, and the need to explain why things should be done or done a certain way.

Boomers fear a time of having to retire before they are financially ready, whether downsizing will hit them and

how it will change their work, if they would qualify for their current job if they had to apply for it, being judged or dismissed by other generations, and of being ignored.

They feel respected when they are: treated politely, their opinions are asked and taken, acknowledged for contributions, listened to, not overlooked, formally recognized, thanked for a job well done, communicated to according to the hierarchy, and recognized according to their authority.

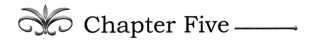 Chapter Five ⎯⎯⎯

The Entrepreneurial Generation X

Every generation is shaped by the cultural and political events of their youth. Like the Baby Boomers, Gen X grew up in a time of change on many domestic and international fronts.

The nuclear accident that occurred on April 26, 1986 at the Chernobyl Nuclear Power Plant in Ukraine released large quantities of radioactive particles into the atmosphere over much of Europe and the January 28, 1986 crash of the space shuttle Challenger three months earlier resulting in the deaths of all seven crew members shook up this generation's beliefs about the absolute safety of technology. These events, juxtaposed with the coming of age of the personal computer, video games, and the internet, presented this generation with a caution-anticipation conflict over the benefits of technology. This led to a generation that sees technology as not necessarily to be feared but neither to be adopted without evidence that it will improve the way we work or live.

Generation X has one foot in the new technology and digital age and one foot in the old analog and industrial age creating a generation that is comfortable in both ages with skills that make Gen Xs both effective leaders and entrepreneurs.

Gen X survived inflation, recession, threat of Canada's downfall due to Quebec referendums, fall of the Berlin Wall, and environmental disasters. Socially, they were the first true generation of divorce, two income families and the latch-key experience of spending time alone until parents returned home from work at the end of the day. They were the first generation to truly be impacted by the AIDS epidemic, requiring a rewrite of social conventions around dating and sex. The happy-go-lucky childhood most Baby Boomers experienced was replaced by cold reality for Generation X.

This created a skeptical, "I will believe it when I see it", "Prove it to me" generation.

A Great Education Leads to No Work

Generation X was a generation that attended university in great numbers compared to previous generations. There were several reasons for this, but two major influences stand out:

Generation X was the first generation to be taught by teachers who for the first time came from a cadre of university scholars versus teaching certificate holders. The teachers of Generation X saw a university degree as the Holy Grail and encouraged teenagers to apply to

university and set themselves up for what they perceived to be a great future. Students talented in technology and skilled trades found themselves in university instead of an education program that matched their passions.

As well, the parents of Generation X had struggled to have the opportunity to attend university and, if attended, often attained a degree through evening, weekend or even distance learning classes. They saw university educated adults succeeding in the work world and wanted that guaranteed future for their children. They thought if their children attended university right out of high school they would be prepared for a well-paid work future.

Unfortunately, due to the downturn in the economy, the overabundance of Baby Boomers in the workplace and a mismatch between education gained and work opportunities, Generation X gained degrees but could not find work related to their fields. They found themselves living with their parents and working at McDonalds (giving the rise to the term McJobs). Generation X's expectations were not met and the overwhelming disappointment of being shut out of the workforce led to a skeptical, pragmatic philosophy.

Generation X's dual income parents created independent children who could work alone and make independent decisions. These Generation X characteristics, coupled with their need to find employment, led to Generation X being the largest per capita group of entrepreneurs of all four generations. They created the work they wanted to do through free agency work or by starting organizations of their own.

Due to their independent, entrepreneurial bent, Gen Xs have little patience with the process, politics and activities of Boomers that do not lead to specific results and outcomes. A Boomer can easily be perceived as busy but ineffective by a pragmatic results-oriented Gen X.

Life Work Balance

Having seen the Boomer generation downsized during recessionary times, Gen Xs see their work as only one part of who they are. Their self-esteem is defined not primarily by their job title, but also by their productivity and documentable success. To this end, Gen Xs are less impressed by authority or seniority, and value skills and expertise that help them keep their career moving.

This generation does not expect stability in the workplace. They expect they may have many jobs in several organizations. Therefore mobility of skills and documentable success is vital.

Loyalty

Traditionalists are loyal to their organization, Baby Boomers to their divisions, and Gen Xs to their managers. This means that if a Gen X's supervisor moves to a different company, the subordinate might go as well if the opportunity presents itself, especially if their relationship with their supervisor is informal and collegial. Working for a manager that they can respect and learn from is more important than staying with the organization. Gen Xs do not see job change as a stigma or stall as most Traditionalists or Boomers would, but as an occasional act necessary to build a career.

How Gen Xs See Themselves

In corporate workshops I have conducted over the past several years, I have asked Boomers, Gen Xs and Gen Ys to explain to the other generations in the room what people need to know about them, what their challenges and fears are and what others can do to help them feel respected in the job.

Here are some Generation X's reflections:

We don't want to be overlooked in the jump between Boomers and Generation Y, we are different and have a unique identity. We need to feel that there is a reason to do the work or attend the meeting, not just because the team has always done it that way. Give us individual work and it will get done. Save us the plaques and certificates of recognition, give us bonuses and extra holidays. We don't need to be best friends with our workmates, just polite and professional with each other. We don't need the latest technology if there is no real improvement in results.

We are challenged by work life balance, new technology and communicating with the other generations.

We are concerned about being overlooked by someone younger in the workplace, the lack of future security in pension and social systems, a lack of future opportunity for our individual work with Boomers staying in the workplace longer and Gen Ys coming in.

We feel respected when we are asked for input or feedback and we can be open about our opinions, when we are

acknowledged or thanked in a genuine way, when we are considered as an equal by management, and allowed to do our job in an autonomous way.

Compare these comments with those in the previous and next chapter to get a better idea of the fears and challenges that are unique to each generation.

Chapter Six ———

The Newer Faster Generation Y

Depending on the demographer, Generation Y began somewhere between 1977 and 1982 and range from teenagers to those in their early 30s in our workplaces today. This generation has been also called Net Generation, Millennials, the iGeneration, and even Generation@.

In many wealthy countries, the 1980s and 1990s were a period of rapidly falling birthrates. Generation Y as a Canadian group, is smaller than the Boomers but larger than Generation X. Although Generation Y is not the smallest generation of the four generations in the Canadian workplace today, they do come from the smallest family size.

It is further interesting to note in Russia, Canada and the United States, Generation Y is relatively large, while in southern Europe and Japan, Generation Y is dramatically smaller than any of its predecessor generations.

The Generation of the Child

UNESCO proclaimed 1979 as the International Year of the Child. This proclamation was intended to draw attention to problems that affected children throughout the world, including malnutrition and lack of access to education. These efforts culminated in the Convention on the Rights of the Child in 1989 which was followed by the International Decade for a Culture of Peace and Non-violence for the Children of the World (2001 to 2010). Globally, issues related to children were at the forefront of policy, news and societal consciousness. This global focus on the child led to domestic and local child-centered policies in education and social issues.

Such policies were scarcely thought of when the other generations were growing up. Traditionalists were raised in parent-centered families where the parents made decisions that were in the best interest of the parents. Baby Boomers and Gen Xs were raised in family-centered systems where parents, with occasional input from children, made decisions in the best interest of the entire family unit. Gen Ys, specifically those who were raised in families of one or two children, were raised in child-centered systems. Parents of Generation Y focused their attention, time, energy and finances on the needs, wants and safety of their children. This focus has resulted in helicopter parents, the self-inflation movement, the assumption of voice, and the need for constant feedback.

Helicopter Parents and the Programmed Gen Y

Consider these three situations:

- In a program called "Careers Unlimited" presented by the Regina Business and Professional Women Organization (BPW Regina) in Saskatchewan, Canada hundreds of high school girls are matched with business and professional women to discuss career opportunities, the educational path required and the pros and cons for each profession. The young women have opportunities to ask questions from the resource women during this school sanctioned event. Over the past 15 years there has been a gradual shift to more mothers attending this event with their daughters and the mothers asking more questions.

- Consider this excerpt from the 'Parents' page of an orientation week publication produced by Queen's University in Kingston, Canada: *"As an adult, your student has primary responsibility for interacting with the university and he/she is directly responsible for managing his/her education (including knowing and following university policies and procedures, seeking academic support, paying fees, etc.)."* It is further interesting to note there is also a parents' guide available to help direct parents in how they can continue to hover over their adult child to graduation at age 22.

- A Manager gets a phone call from the parent of a Gen Y staff member. Her child is sick and will not be in to work today.

These situations highlight the fact that Gen Ys have been programmed from the earliest age to have their parents involved in every decision they make and this input from parents or a trusted advisor is essential in their decision-making process. They have an expectation that their parents will figure it out and let them know what to do, how it will work and not only co-decide but take co-action. For an adult Gen Y living at home, having a parent make their medical appointments or call in sick for them to work is neither illogical nor uncommon.

The childhood activities of many Gen Ys were programmed from their waking up until their bedtime. Reasons parents relate for this regimentation includes the desire to keep children busy and out of mischief, to give children well-rounded programmed activities, and to fulfill their children's expectations. This also meant there was less time for children to experience free play where children identify options, learn to make decisions, lead others and create teams.

The Self-Inflation Movement

Generation Y was reared on a healthy dose of self-esteem. Parents and the teachers of Gen Y students raised Gen Y in an encouraging and confidence building environment. Gen Y learned from teachers, parents and society that they could be anything they set their mind to be and achieve whatever they want to achieve. Unfortunately Gen Ys often want these great dreams immediately and they often have no plan or process to make it happen. They have immense expectations without a practical or realistic roadmap.

The upside of high self-esteem (how people think and feel about themselves in the world) is that they feel competent,

understood, worthy and appreciated. This leads to higher productivity and innovation. Those with low self-esteem often feel unworthy and incompetent, leading sometimes to a person hiding their weaknesses and taking both positive and negative feedback poorly.

The *self-inflation* movement is the concept of raising children to feel good about themselves to the extent that positive feedback is given for good, mediocre and even poor performance. The self-inflation movement results in children entering the adult world with an unrealistic view of their abilities and a lack of preparation for negative feedback on their performance.

As a mediocre golfer, I am all for receiving the 'most honest' award, but all the golfers involved know it stands for last place and therefore is a sympathy prize. However, when children receive awards for merely being a member of a group, or receive a ribbon for coming in 15ᵗʰ of 15 competitors, there are significant consequences as they build their belief system about what to expect as an adult.

Due to the concern for the self-esteem of the child, society, parents and educators have protected the Gen Y from consequence of their negative actions or lack of action.

Consider this situation in Alberta:

In September 2012, chemistry and physics high school teacher, Lynden Dorval was fired by the Edmonton Public School Board for insisting that students who did not complete assignments or missed exams receive a zero grade. He said *"High school students are not little kids. It's time to become an adult and take responsibility for your own actions".* His practice was to show the student how a

zero mark would impact their overall grade and then leave it up to the student to come to him to negotiate a rewrite or completion of the assignment. His resistance to enforcing the school's 'no zero policy' regardless of the initiative of the student to complete their work led to his dismissal.

After considerable media and citizen debate, the Edmonton Public School Board unveiled a new draft assessment policy to include a possible grade of zero. "We make it really explicit in the policy that teachers are expected to have students do their work, students are expected to do their work, and that grades can range from D to A, and from zero to 100," said EPSB Chair, Sarah Hoffman. The proposed policy outlines expectations of both staff and students. If approved, every school in the district will be required to abide by the new policy. "It's important to ... be fair and consistent so that no matter which school, or which school division you come from, you know that an 85 is an 85."

In the draft policy, achievement is defined as "how well a student demonstrates grade level learner outcomes represented by a grade. Grades are represented by letters A, B, C, D; percentages 0-100%; or the descriptors: not yet demonstrating to demonstrating in-depth understanding."

It is interesting that in Generation Y's time, we have to put in writing that we expect students to actually do the work, to accomplish goals, and be held accountable. In the workplace, real deadlines exist and there are not always opportunities for 'do-overs'. There are real consequences for not showing up and getting the work done. There will be little love for a Gen Y in the workplace who doesn't take responsibility for their lack of performance.

Children who were protected from the negative consequences of their poor performance are not the only students to have been affected by these types of policies and actions. Consider the academically proficient or scholastically excellent student who does not gain increased positive self-esteem with his success because his fellow students who perform less well than he are treated with the same positive acknowledgement.

Take that reality into the workplace. If a Gen Y does not have a negative consequence following poor or non-performance, it reinforces that it is permissible to not perform. Also, for performing colleagues, the non-performance of another can negatively impact their level of job satisfaction and commitment and even foster resentment towards the non-performing Gen Y. "Why does he get away with poor performance when they expect me to be diligent? Who does he think he is?"

Assumption of Voice

Gen Ys not only come from smaller families than previous generations, their opinion was asked for and listened to in their family units. Parents of this generation want to be friends with their children, and see a congenial relationship as a sign of successfully parenting. This collegiality was encouraged from the earliest age, with parents asking for input from their children for all types of decisions. This effect was particularly predominant in single parent families of one or two children, where the parent allowed and encouraged their children to act as the second adult in the home.

Gen Ys come into the workforce with the collegial mindset, and are confused and annoyed that those in the workplace who are more senior in age or experience do

not ask for their ideas and may not listen to their opinion when it is offered.

"Who do these kids think they are?" Traditionalists and Boomers remember their earliest days of employment when they didn't ask a question, speak up, or speak out. They find the immediate and assertive contributions of Gen Ys both confusing and annoying.

Generation Ys, as children, were invited into the adult world and treated as partners in decision making, not as offspring. Gen Ys therefore see themselves equal in decision-making authority and power to those a generation or more older than they and expect equitable relationships with superiors in the workplace.

This abdication of decision making by parents has led to disappointment by Gen Ys as they begin working in what they were told by their recruiting manager or human resource professional was an equitable and inclusive environment. Ironically, the Boomer parent that asked their children what they would like for dinner is the same Boomer colleague who feels annoyed with the forward outspoken Gen Y in their workplace.

Why and Why Not?

Another effect of self-inflation and the desire for a collegial parent-child relationship is Generation Y's resistance to hearing the answer 'no' to one of their ideas or an idea or direction that is contrary to their thinking.

Traditionalists and Boomers often do what they are requested to do because the one asking is their manager. Gen Xs will follow instructions but if they disagree with the validity of the direction, they may strategically negotiate or persuade their manager to change the plan. Gen Ys will do what they agree with and what makes sense to them. If the plan doesn't make sense or they don't want to do it, they are more than willing to challenge their supervisor regarding the request or simply ignore the task.

Unless a manager can explain the rationale for doing something, Gen Ys will often resist taking action. 'Because we do it that way,' or 'you don't need to know that' are responses that might work with Boomers and even Gen Xs, but will get little buy-in from a Gen Y.

On the flipside, if a Gen Y goes to their manager with an idea or request and the manager is not receptive, the Gen Y is more likely than a member of any other generation to then approach their manager's manager with the same item. Such an act is seen as a very negative thing in the Boomer and Traditionalist world and often tagged with the negative comment of 'going over your manager's head'. However, this same act may be seen strategic to a Gen X world and absolutely logical to a Gen Y.

Feedback

Gen Ys have experienced not only positive feedback for mediocre or poor work, they received that feedback frequently. Where Gen X can be left alone for periods of

time, many Gen Ys think they have been forgotten if no one checks out how they are doing from time to time. That time to time for a Boomer could be every three months, for a Gen X every three weeks and for a Gen Y, every three hours.

In the workplace, Gen Ys are used to constant communication, whether in person or via technology. They have an expectation of close supervision and instantaneous supportive feedback.

Traditionalists, as we discussed earlier, had a 'no news is good news' perspective on feedback and performance evaluation. Boomers felt that they needed more formality and the yearly performance review was born. Gen Xs care not only what their manager thinks but also what everyone above, below and beside them thinks and birthed the 360 degree performance evaluation. Gen Ys have an expectation of frequent and immediate evaluation of their performance, even though they are more challenged with negative feedback than the other generations. In Chapter Nine we will discuss a specific feedback technique that works with all generations, but specifically with Gen Y.

Globally Connected, Uninformed and Uncritical

Gen Y grew up with the expansion of global communications, making it possible to have friends around the world. Their global and local friends can be extremely diverse and this generation appears to be the most comfortable with people from other cultures and faiths.

But the instantly accessible, data rich world of technology comes with challenges for Gen Ys. The extreme content proliferation contained on websites and in blogs is a mine field to navigate for reliable, accurate information. Much web information is opinion based and it is difficult for readers without critical thinking skills to discern what is credible information or which edition of multiple versions is accurate. Gen Ys receive much of their information from others who may or may not be disseminating accurate facts. Instead of peer reviewed articles, blogs and sites such as Wikipedia are seen as reliable sources for research.

The Digital Comfort Zone

If I came to Canada only speaking the Ukrainian language, I would learn English but Ukrainian would always be my go-to language for discussion with others who knew that language. I would probably prefer to read fiction or work materials in Ukrainian. I would perhaps continue to think in Ukrainian and translate in my head from my mother tongue to my second language.

My comfort zone would be Ukrainian and it would the most comfortable language in which to converse. Over time I would become more and proficient in English, but would still have a warm feeling when I could speak my first language. Technology is like that.

As Baby Boomer and Traditionalists learn to use digital technology efficiently, it is as if they are learning it as a second language after their first language of analog. Gen Ys were born after the analog world of VCRs, 8-track cassettes, Gestetner machines and multi-page carbon forms.

Just as Ukrainian parents who speak English as a second language raise their children to speak English as a first language, the three previous generations have created the technology of digital and raised Gen Ys to embrace it. Gen Ys can't understand the wistfulness of the 8-track tape any more than a Canadian born understands why his mother keeps drifting back into Ukrainian. The first three generations had to learn digital as a second language and Gen Ys grew up speaking digital as their mother tongue.

In an analog world, we function in process. Consider a movie on VHS. You watch it from beginning to end. In a digital world, a DVD allows you to skip over what you don't want to see, review the interesting parts and watch the segments in any order you wish. Certainly, with enough time, you could painstakingly rewind and replay a VHS tape, but few Gen Ys would have the patience for it. Time is something that this generation is not willing to waste. The axiom 'patience is a virtue' has been lost.

Consensus and Group Work

Generation Y, like Generation X, grew up alone as parents worked. But unlike Gen Xs who grew up isolated, Gen Ys were connected to others through the technology of email, text messaging, cell phones, chat rooms and social networking sites. This constant group connection did not create the independent thinkers and workers of the Gen X generation, but ones that prefer to work collaboratively and depend on input from others before making decisions.

How Gen Y See Themselves

In corporate workshops I have conducted over the past several years, I have asked Boomers, Gen Xs and Gen Ys to explain to the other generations in the room what people need to know about them, what their challenges and fears are, and what others can do to help them feel respected in the job.

Here are some Generation Y reflections:

We see ourselves as lifelong learners and we want to be challenged.

Our challenges include: expecting respect but not always getting it, wanting to introduce new methods but being frustrated with the 'this is how it has always been' mentality, being adaptable and open to new methods while others seem to feel threatened, learning the expected rules and etiquette of the workplace, not being treated as a peer because of our age, and having others assume we know and constantly use all the latest technology.

We fear getting an education but not finding a job, being judged on the basis of our age, being expected to know all the latest technology, and losing upward mobility due to the slowing of the retirement of Baby Boomers.

We feel respected when: there is team sharing and others are open to all ideas, others are critical of the idea but not the individual and all ideas have merit, there is proper communication and feedback, ideas are heard and implemented, we are included in processes regarding planning or changes, and a job well done is acknowledged.

Chapter Seven ────

Why Occasionally None of This Matters

When we are not of a particular group, we see that group homogenously. When we are part of a group we see our identity more specifically. This ability to generalize creates opportunities for us to create stereotypes – where we take an example of one or a few people of a certain group and generalize that all people of that group are similarly motivated, repulsed, interested and so on.

Research on specific groups can itself create stereotypes that limit managers in leading effectively. For example, think of the research that has been done in the issues tied to the four-generation workforce. What do Gen Xs and Gen Ys want in the workplace? Certainly there is data that has been collected and analyzed, but even in this book, readers must be cautious about how research might in itself create stereotypes that limit how they attract and retain individuals from the four generations.

Generational information is only one of many ways people are diverse. All areas of diversity must be considered when managing others. Let's consider five specific examples relating to Generation Y. If a Gen Y grew up on a farm, on a First Nations reserve, is an immigrant, from a large family, or from an entrepreneurial family the worldview of the typical Gen Y we discussed in the previous chapter may not be accurate.

Consider a Gen X who grew up in another country and experienced financial chaos or a lack of personal physical safety. That Gen X may be inclined to behave like a member of the Traditionalist generation who also came out of economic chaos and instability, specifically the depression era and World War Two. This Gen X may well be less inclined to clash with the corporate culture and accept any opportunity that is before them gratefully – as did members of the Traditionalist generation.

Consider a Gen Y who grew up on a reserve as a member of a First Nation. He may not feel connected to the economic opportunities other Gen Ys have experienced. He may have grown up in a similar societal reality to a typical Gen X where governments promised change but didn't deliver. It is possible that his parents were unable to provide the digital technology other youth his age owned. As schools on reserves are not funded as fully as schools under provincial jurisdictions, it is possible that a Gen Y who grew up on reserve had very limited access to digital technology. It is possible that high speed internet service or even efficient cell service didn't exist where he lived. If he comes from a family with high

unemployment this may also increase the likelihood that he sees the world with the skepticism of the typical Gen X.

Being raised in an entrepreneurial family where you were responsible for customer service or financial items impacts the belief system of a Gen Y. Not taking the appropriate actions at the appropriate times could mean loss economically for the family. A Gen Y growing up in an entrepreneurial family is more likely to be aware how their parents make money and what they sacrifice to make that income.

A Gen Y who grew up on a family farm, especially mixed farming where animals are involved, has a strong awareness of the relationship between their behaviour and consequence. Something seemingly inconsequential such as not closing a fence gate could lead to dire consequences such as livestock escaping and being killed by passing vehicles on the road. Seeing life come into the world and being responsible for the care of other living beings creates individuals with a keen understanding that it doesn't matter what you would like to do or not do, certain tasks just must be done.

The self-inflation and helicopter parent phenomena cannot exist in a family with six children. In a large family, parents do not have the time or resources to dote upon that many children.

Individuals from middle class to affluent backgrounds, raised in small families from multi-generational European-descent Canadian parents are the most aligned with the generational trends.

⚜ Chapter Eight ⎯⎯

Why We Can't Just Get Along

When we observe another person's behaviour (what they say or do), we add to that input our interpretation (our beliefs and value interpretations) and our intention (what would be our motivation if we were exhibiting the same behaviour) to create what we believe is real. Therefore when we judge the behaviour of others, our judgement is partly based on what they did and partly based on how we see it.

Let's take the example of a manager who is part of the Baby Boomer generation. Suppose that one of his Gen Y employees asks for additional resources – perhaps a new computer – and permission is denied due to budgetary restraints. Not being happy with this result, the Gen Y employee goes over his manager's head and places the

same request with the manager's boss, the regional Vice-President. The manager would no doubt see this behaviour in a negative way. He may conclude that his employee does not respect his managerial role and the hierarchy of the organization.

However, suppose the manager is part of Generation Y. If one of his Generation Y employees was denied such a request for a new computer and that employee went over that manager's head, the manager might see it less negatively. In fact, he might commend his employee for being resourceful. The behaviour of the subordinate has not changed, but the perspective of the supervisor has. So in the eyes of the Generation Y manager the Generation Y subordinate is resourceful, and in the eyes of the Boomer supervisor, the Generation Y employee is insubordinate.

Hierarchy and Formality

There are several areas where our generational interpretation (our beliefs and values developed during the age we were raised) comes into conflict with others in the workplace. The relationship described in the previous paragraphs relates to how we think differently, depending on our generation, about the issue of hierarchy and formality.

Traditionalists raised in parent-centered systems respect hierarchy and the structure of the military-defined organizational chart. This is particularly enforced within the civil service, where a civil servant's role is strictly defined by which documents he is permitted to sign. The rigidity of the military is still seen in Canada's federal civil service where terms such as **officer** as in Corrections Officer and **general** as in Auditor General continue to exist.

Boomers and Gen Xs, who were raised in family-centered systems and look for a relaxing of structure, still have a healthy respect for the hierarchy of the organization and appreciate the clarity of knowing who works for whom and what the parameters and boundaries are that define their role in the workplace. Job descriptions create emotional safety for Baby Boomers and the dotted lines on the organizational chart provide some flexibility.

Gen Ys were raised in non-hierarchical, child-centered systems with low formality requirements both at home and in the education system. Instructors in colleges and universities invite students to call them by their first names, as do the parents of their Gen Y friends. Gen Ys do not necessarily recognize or adhere to the etiquette of the workplace, the rules of interaction, or the culture of the relationships between different levels of power and authority.

So we can see how Boomers can be viewed as inflexible and Gen Ys as disrespectful – depending of course on whose generational lens you are peeking through.

Communication

The Traditionalist says "write me" or "see me", the Boomer says "call me", the Gen X says "email me" and the Gen Y says "text me". Every generation has their preferential communication medium that they are the most comfortable using, even though they are familiar with all. Certainly many Traditionalists text and Gen Ys use the telephone to make calls, however the first inclination is to use our 'go-to' medium.

In Chapter Two, we discussed the new work ethic model. In the segment above we discussed hierarchy. How we

communicate and with whom ties to the work ethic elements of both etiquette and eloquence.

How we do it

When we use our go-to technology it could be efficient or problematic. There are more or less appropriate times to use each communication tool.

When a person needs a quick answer, they are frustrated if the provider of the answer insists on a phone call or an in person meeting, delaying their next action.

However, in complex situations, a series of back and forth texts can add confusion to a matter and a letter or email that encapsulates the entire matter may be a better choice for full understanding by all parties. In conflict-ridden situations, the face-to-face or ear-to-ear of a visit or phone call is more likely to move towards resolution than curt emails and rapid fire texts. There is more information that can be gleaned with body gestures and voice tone to assist both parties in moving toward rapport and resolution.

So all generational groups must take a moment to identify what technology is best in a given situation to aid communication and productivity. If a situation that is text or email based is spiralling out of control, switch immediately to phone or in person communication.

Who we do it with

Gen Ys see that the important thing is to achieve the goal regardless of whom they have to talk to. If the President is in the elevator with them, why not strike while the opportunity presents itself? A Traditionalist or Baby Boomer would respect the lines of authority as defined by

their organizational chart and smile at the President and engage if the President does first. A Gen X might engage in conversation with the President and if the conversation creates an opening to discuss their goals without directly calling for action, a strategic Gen X might take the opportunity to move their agenda along. The direct style of a Gen Y who fully expects the President to be interested in their opinion, to welcome a conversation with them and want to help them as a colleague, may be seen as too forward or even arrogant by other generations.

Advancement

As we discussed in the previous chapter, the self-inflation movement created a generation that sees little value in earning their stripes, climbing the ladder or learning the ropes – all metaphors and beliefs that were embraced by previous generations. Gen Ys were raised in the age of reality television shows such as American Idol and the X Factor, where you could be an unknown today and wealthy or famous tomorrow. Media in its various forms influenced this generation more so than educators or parents. What stars and celebrities think and endorse have a significant impact on how Gen Ys behave. Thanks to self-inflation, this 'it could happen to me and it should' generation has misplaced confidence in their abilities, skill set and value to the organization.

Earlier generations' confidence and competence rose in lockstep, or their competence outran their confidence, but Generation Y's confidence often outstrips their competence. In the chapter following, the Staircase Model explains how to lead Gen Ys to achieve matching competence and confidence in their roles.

Change

Change is seen differently by the four generations. The two older generational groups, Traditionalists and Baby Boomers generally see change as a negative thing. Consider the Baby Boomers who prayed on December 31st, 1999 that their old 286 Mhz computers would survive the Y2K disaster that had been prophesized. Or the Boomer who holds on to her cell phone until she is either mandated to change by her organization, or the phone breaks. The two older generations often also see changing policies, procedures and protocols to mean that the old way of doing things is broken and change should be taken cautiously, if at all. They look to 'budget' change, where minor adjustments can be made to fix the current problem.

For the two younger generations, Generation X and Generation Y, however, change is not seen as a negative thing. It is an opportunity for improvement and innovation. With job change, these two generations do not see the career stall and stigma that older generations perceive. They see job change in a positive light, a pathway to mobility and success, a chance for more meaningful work and an opportunity for professional and personal growth.

Although Gen Xs only welcome change if there is a good reason to do so, Gen Ys equate change with new and exciting developments. They ask "why shouldn't we change?" not "why should we change?" which is the rallying cry of older generations.

In contrast to the two younger generations, the two older generations fundamentally see change in a negative light. Therefore around a board table, the two groups will often

divide down the middle as change is addressed. The older generations will fight for what has been, not only because they might have been part of the old policy development, but because change is uncomfortable. It doesn't feel safe. The younger generations around the table will fight for the new and improved, with little or no commitment to what has been done in the past. Staying with what has been feels stifling and counterproductive.

Another way of looking at the situation is that the two older generations are often reticent to start 'with a blank slate' which feels uncomfortable. The younger generations, on the other hand, feel budgeted change – a little at a time is painfully slow.

Balancing and Blending Personal and Work

Traditionalists have very definite boxes marked work and non-work. Boomers attempt to balance their different boxes, guiltily sneaking a moment for a personal call or email while in the workplace.

Gen Xs may sometimes appear uncommitted to their jobs when they work only the required hours and little more as they seek more balance between their personal and professional lives than Traditionalists and Baby Boomers. Gen Xs are more likely to question workplace expectations, such as long work hours or taking work home, and are more open about their parenting commitments and obligations. Gen Xs justify the intrusion of personal life into their work life because they still get the work done and tasks accomplished.

Gen Xs attempt to balance. Gen Ys see no need to balance because there is no line between work and play – life is one seamless adventure where work is a part of life, as

are friends, family, Facebook and favourite hobbies. That means there is no reason for their non-work life not to interact with their work life. One area of their life (such as work) does not supersede another. Gen Ys therefore do not perceive there to be an issue with personal calls, texts or social networking while they are 'at work'.

Flexibility and Negotiation

Gen Ys believe in working smarter and not harder. They believe there is often an easier, quicker and more efficient way of doing a task and sometimes they are correct. They want the flexibility of working when, where and how they wish and don't see that putting the hours in at a desk or adhering to predetermined start and end times as necessary to get the work completed.

In concert with these ideas, Gen Ys are more likely to see all workplace policies as open to negotiation. Traditionalists and Boomers would never have questioned work times as automatically negotiable. Even Gen Xs see flex time as a hard earned benefit, not an entitlement.

Asking Questions

Generation Y has been jokingly referred to as 'Gen Why' because Gen Ys often ask the question "why"? First and second year apprentices (many who are Gen Ys) in the skilled trades are often supervised and mentored by ticketed journeypersons who are Traditionalists and Boomers. These mentors find that Gen Y apprentices will frequently ask them why they do something or do it a certain way. Older employees often feel that they are being challenged because in their apprenticeship days they would never have dared ask a supervising journeyman

why he used a different process than the one the apprentice learned at trade school. The Gen Y doesn't believe that their behavior is disrespectful, but the older employee often perceives it that way. Gen Ys were raised to question everything and query anything that didn't make sense to them.

Gen Ys expect relationships in the workplace to mirror the collegial relationships they have with their parents and are confused why others in the workplace may want a more formal hierarchical relationship. They are accused of not respecting older generations while at the same time, they feel they are not respected for their knowledge and other traits they bring to the job. Ironically, asking questions can sometimes lead to answers or solutions that are actually more efficient and effective.

Loyalty and Longevity

In a study discussed in the *Journal of Diversity Management*, 5057 individuals from the four generational groups were surveyed using the Rokeach Value Survey of 18 values. The third top value for Boomers (after honest and responsible) was loyalty. The fourth top value for Gen Xs (after honest, responsible, and capable) was loyalty. The sixth top value for Gen Ys (after honest, responsible, loving, independent, and ambitious) was loyalty.

Each generation values loyalty.

Gen Xs value being seen as capable, working with capable people and working for a capable manager more than loyalty. If their manager is not capable or if they are surrounded by incompetence, they will look for other work opportunities.

Gen Ys have higher values for independence and ambition than loyalty. If they feel that there are too many unnecessary rules and there is no leeway for negotiating those rules, they will be dissatisfied. Likewise, if they see that there is little upward mobility or opportunity to grow, learn or make a difference in their current work situation, they will be dissatisfied and look for other job opportunities.

We see this research play out in the following ways:

Traditionalists stay with an organization as long as the employer-employee relationship of 'you take care of me and I do a good job for you' remains intact. Traditionalists interpret job change as a failure on the employee's part and that there is stigma attached to having multiple jobs on a resume. Boomers also often see job change in a negative way as they aspire to remain with one organization for their career and climb the ladder. It takes either an exceptional opportunity to tempt them to move on or extreme negative work conditions for them to search out a new opportunity.

Gen Ys are surprised when Boomers who are extremely unhappy in their work continue to hang in there, just because retirement may be around the corner. Boomers are surprised that Gen Ys will change jobs if they don't think the manager is straightforward enough with the staff.

In the next chapter we will discuss how leaders can manage the behaviourial differences outlined in this chapter.

～ Chapter Nine ——

Managing Generation Y

As we have discussed in earlier chapters, every generational group has preferences in work style and work environment.

Consider this real life situation:

A health care consultant has a research project with a deadline and stated deliverable – in this case a report to be presented to a health care district about an upcoming facility change. The consultant is a Baby Boomer/Gen X cusper and her team of five members are all Gen Ys. She outlined the project, key tasks, rules of engagement and then posted the opportunity through her on-line community. Within a couple of days, she had her team identified and began work. The team accessed the research in the medium they wished, wrote when they wished and where they wished, and posted to the mutual

cloud their research findings, conclusions and recommendations. The consultant felt that her team was excellent and the project was not encumbered by any generational conflict. The consultant did not ask for her team members to work her way, she worked theirs. They worked how they wanted, where they wanted, when they wanted, with the technology they wished, on a project that they found meaningful.

However, we know that all work is not going to fall into a neat little box as above where we can meet our employees completely on their terms, so other strategies are required.

Loyalty Through Authentic Leadership

As we discussed in the previous chapter, loyalty is a value for all generations, however loyalty and staying with the organization are not synonymous to a Gen Y. Traditionalists and Baby Boomers are loyal to an organization and stay there long term if the employer-employee relationship continues. Gen Xs are loyal to their team and manager and as long as their manager is competent and creates opportunities for a Gen X's growth and advancement, he or she will continue to be loyal to their manager and are likely to remain with the organization.

But Gen Ys retention relates more to the authenticity of their leaders than the organization itself. Gen Ys value integrity and commit to those who display it. Behaviours such as doing what you say you will, honouring commitments, shouldering blame and sharing success show consistent, predictable leadership that appeals to Gen Ys. They are willing to follow those who they find compelling and could change jobs at a moment's notice to be on a team that they find more meaningful with a

leader that they respect. Although this quick willingness to move may be seen by previous generations as demonstrating a lack of consistency, dependability or loyalty, it can be used in a leader's favour. A transparent leader that demonstrates both skills and experience and a willingness to be courageous and insightful can influence Gen Ys to join their team and remain engaged.

Recognition

For Gen Ys who stay with your organization, consider how you show recognition. The value of 'time served' in an organization is not synonymous for all generational groups.

As Gen Ys have less appreciation for earning their stripes, climbing the ropes or buttressing up egos, employee recognition awards banquets will be met with cynicism and poor attendance by Gen Ys. While giving a Traditionalist or Boomer a plaque commemorating their years of commitment to an organization may be seen as an important symbol of dedication to the organization, consider something more encompassing so as to include the Gen Ys.

If award ceremonies are included in your corporate culture, think about creating awards that recognize longevity, but also productivity, profitability and other measurements of value that might resonate with a Gen Y.

Establish a Work Ethic

As we discussed in the second chapter, establishing a code of behaviour may be an essential key to managing different generations.

Traditionally, the emphasis in ethics has been on avoiding harm, fulfilling contracts, and obeying the law. But avoiding the bad is not the same as pursuing the good, and ethical standards at work can be supplemented with another standard; a virtuous standard that includes the areas detailed into the new work ethic model in Chapter Two.

According to J. Gallos in the book *Business Leadership,* a virtuous standard can serve as a fixed point to guide individual and organizational behaviours in times of ambiguity, turbulence, or high-velocity change. Certainly the multi-generational workplace of the 21st century is just that - one of turbulence, ambiguity and change.

All employees should be held to the same standard or code, however leaders must ensure they are seen as role models. Leaders set the tone for an organization and its employees, and therefore must ensure that they consistently demonstrate the espoused work ethics of their organization.

Creating a code of ethics or code of behaviour in the workplace (work ethic) is about examining, questioning, exploring, deciding and committing. Members of the organization have to live with their codes, a consequence that can be quite difficult. This means that the code must make sense for everyone who might have to adhere to it. It must align with an organization's values and principles, as well as the values and principles of the individual members. (It must also align with the values and principles of individuals' professions. Without clarity on this issue, an ethical conflict or dilemma may arise if the organization desires one thing but that outcome is in violation with the ethics of a professional code of conduct.)

Without a code of ethics, behaviours of others are judged by our personal interpretation of values. If enough conflict arises, organizations resort to mandating regulations on how we communicate and behave.

Let's look at the work ethic model we explored in Chapter Two:

The New 'Work Ethic'

Again, the six key areas where we have expectations of ourselves and others in the workplace are:

1. Education
2. Experience
3. Enthusiasm and Energy
4. Endurance and Effort
5. Eloquence
6. Etiquette

To develop your own code of ethics and define your new work ethic for your team or organization, take time to explore, examine, question, decide and commit to answers to areas such as:

1. Education: reaching out to learn in formal and informal ways to be able to deliver higher value to the employer, searching and embracing opportunities to learn from others and be mentored, or seeking out knowledge outside of learning opportunities designated by a manager.

2. Experience: searching out opportunities to try new tasks and take on new responsibilities, transferring these experiences into wisdom that can be used in similar or dissimilar situations, or successfully mentoring others.

3. Enthusiasm and Energy: having a daily positive attitude, or managing physical health to ensure energy to do the required tasks with acceptable speed and accuracy.

4. Endurance and Effort: willingness to continue on task to completion, pushing through difficult, complicated or new tasks until the task is completed, developing new knowledge or skills, or patiently completing mundane tasks that may be considered a mismatch for skill and knowledge levels.

5. Eloquence: communicating persuasively in written, verbal and in person formats, or working with diverse individuals.

6. Etiquette: knowing what levels of an organization an issue should be addressed with, or successfully determining which format of communication (text, written, telephone or in person) is required for the level of complexity and conflict in the communication.

Find the Performance Issue

Success for an employee is a joint effort with their manager. But when we are new to the world of work, we often do not know why we are not being successful and therefore we cannot tell our manager what we need to improve.

This leaves it to the supervisor to try to unbundle the employee's behaviour and to determine what is the cause of the poor performance.

Consider the following guide for narrowing down what is not working with your Gen Y employee.

What is the unsatisfactory performance or behaviour?

Is it worth your time and attention?

Move on.

Does the employee know their performance is not satisfactory? Are they getting effective feedback?

Does the employee know what is supposed to be done? By when? Standards?

Provide effective and specific feedback. What is wrong? What do you want to see change?

Provide clear expectations.

Are there obstacles beyond the employees' control?

Remove obstacles.

Do they know how to do it?

Provide training.

Do negative consequences follow good performance, or do positive consequences follow non-performance?

Could the employee do it if they wanted to?

Change consequences.

Terminate employee.

MARTRAIN
Jeanne Martinson

Question One: Is it worth your time and effort?

When we are working with people different than ourselves, sometimes we confuse performance with preference. Compare the employee's performance issue with the code of ethics (work ethic) you have determined. Are they violating what you have determined in your team or organization to be your code of conduct? Is this about you or them? Are they getting it done but just not your way? If after that contemplation, you determine that it is not about performance, let the issue go.

If yes, it is a performance issue, move on to the next question.

Question Two: Does the employee know that their performance is not satisfactory? Are they getting effective feedback?

Do not assume that it is common sense that the employee would know what to do. We have discussed earlier that common sense is not all that common, we all have different perspectives of what should be done and how it should be done. A leader must be able to clearly communicate what has to be done, by when and by what methods. A supervisor often thinks that they have given clear feedback to an employee, but the message has not gotten through.

In the next segment we will discuss feedback and how to ensure that your Gen Y employee 'gets' the message clearly.

If you are not absolutely certain that you have given clear and effective feedback, this is your next step. However, if the employee has received effective feedback and the performance issue still exists, ask the third question.

Question Three: Does the employee know what is supposed to be done, by when and by what standards?

Again, often we think that this is just common sense, or that the employee will have figured it out on their own. Gen Y employees need to have details and clear instructions more so than any other generation. They are excellent at sourcing information faster than any other generation, but they were also restricted in their free play as children which is where we develop the skill to identify effective processes and problem solve. If you have given clear, specific information and the performance is still poor, move on to question four.

Question Four: Are there obstacles beyond the employee's control?

This is particularly important for managing Gen Ys. If a Gen Y is given a task but there are political, resource or time barriers to their success, they will become demotivated quickly. Like other generations, they may or may not tell you what the barriers are. However unlike other generations who may work around the barriers, eliminate the barriers or complain about the barriers to others, Gen Ys might just walk away and you will never know what was the cause for their departure.

Ask if there is anything that you can do to help them succeed in this task and if there is anything or anyone that is hindering their progress. If you determine that there are no barriers, move on to question five.

Question Five: Do they know how to do it?

Again this sounds like an obvious common sense given. Of course the person would know how to do it. But

perhaps they received no training or poor training on the task. Ask if they know how to do the task, and more importantly have them describe it step by step to you to ensure mutual understanding.

Question Six: Do negative consequences follow good performance or do positive consequences follow non-performance?

This question is particularly relevant for managing Gen Ys. We discussed in earlier chapters the effect of the self-inflation movement and its demotivating impact on performing Gen Ys who see their colleagues poorly perform but be rewarded. However the impact on the poor performing Gen Y who has no negative consequence reinforces their childhood upbringing of self-inflation and encourages them to non-perform because in their perspective it just doesn't matter if you do a good job or not. This is one area where leaders need to be extremely diligent. When an employee performs, you need to notice and comment. When they do not perform, you need to notice and give immediate negative feedback.

Assuming that there are appropriate consequences to negative and positive performance, move to the next and final question.

Question Seven: Could the employee do it if they wanted to?

If the employee has the training, appropriate feedback, appropriate consequences, direction and knowledge yet continues to poorly perform, it is time to use progressive discipline to document (which this guide assists you with by providing a process), discipline and ultimately perhaps even terminate.

Give Effective Feedback

Every generation wants feedback and they want it as clearly communicated as possible. But Gen Ys especially need clear feedback as they simply do not have the experience to understand vague summarizing directions.

Many managers have been trained with the 'feedback sandwich' where you provide positive feedback followed by negative feedback and finish up with a dash of good feedback before you finish the conversation. This feedback strategy often fails due to the factor of 'recency' where the employee most strongly remembers the last thing that was said to them and the 'averaging' factor where an employee can tell themselves that overall they are doing a good job.

The good news/bad news/good news of the feedback sandwich does not work effectively with any of the generational groups and it is particularly risky with Gen Y employees. Gen Ys are not used to negative feedback where they are to be held responsible for the consequence of the behaviour so they are most likely of all four of the generational groups to minimize the negative feedback and focus on the positive feedback at the beginning and end of the conversation.

Managers generally dislike giving negative feedback. That is only human nature. However by giving confusing feedback or no feedback at all, the manager is setting up the employee for failure and the organization for possible legal issues because they have not given the employee an opportunity to truly learn how they could improve.

Let's discuss a clear positive and negative feedback process that works with all generational groups.

Positive Feedback

Describe the behaviour you observed (specifically and when), the immediate consequence of that behaviour and the further impact of the consequence. For example, "Yesterday, when you asked everyone for their opinion during the meeting, that led all the members of the group to feel their expertise counted. That positively impacted the team in that they will speak up more often. This helps our organization by increasing the number of new ideas."

It is describing the ongoing impacts of the behaviour that affects the employee. Often individuals do not realize how their actions impact their team or their organization. You will notice that we first describe the behaviour and then consequences and impacts.

It is vital that you focus on behaviour (what you saw or heard) not vague interpretation, particularly when discussing behaviour you wish to see them change. "When you interrupted me earlier" is behaviour, "You were rude" is an interpretation of that behaviour. An employee will not connect intellectually with your interpretation of their behaviour, only emotionally. So they feel defensive and badly but don't understand what they specifically did that they can change.

It is also important that you are specific and not general. For example, to ask an employee to be "more friendly" when they already see themselves as a friendly person is counterproductive and increases defensiveness in the employee. Asking them to "smile when a customer comes up to the desk" is clear behaviour-based feedback.

Negative Feedback

Positive feedback is given to increase self-esteem in the employee and to ensure that they continue the behaviour that you have identified as positive. Negative feedback is given to communicate to an employee that you want them to begin a new behaviour that they are not exhibiting, change or stop a behaviour that is having negative consequences and impacts.

Describe the negative behaviour you have observed, its negative consequences and impacts. The deeper you can go on with impacts, the more the employee will see what they are doing is negatively affecting others. With Gen Ys particularly, the negative impact has to be driven home because they have less experience in the workplace and the negative impact that they are causing with their behaviour is less obvious to them.

Then describe the positive behaviour you wish to see the Gen Y exhibit, followed by the positive consequences and impacts to the organization and team. Everyone wants to be liked in the workplace. Gen Ys often feel that they are not respected at work due to their age and so connecting performance to the respect and caring from their colleagues is important. Here is an example: "When you automatically discard information from your hard drive, this leads to others not being able to access important data when you are not here. This leads to staff feeling incompetent and our customers not being well served. Those two outcomes lead to a possible decrease in client retention and job satisfaction. What I would like you to rather do is to leave information accessible to others. This would lead to other staff being able to access info immediately. This would lead to staff being able to be efficient and deliver good service."

Match Competence to Confidence

Due to the self-inflation movement we discussed earlier, some Gen Ys have a mismatch between their confidence and competence levels. They believe they can and should be taking on more responsibility quicker than their leader might think they should. Many Boomers and even Gen Xs climbed slowly up the ladder and have an expectation that Gen Ys should and would experience the same career speed.

Regardless of expectations of the past, today's leader should increase the authority and responsibility of their Gen Ys as soon as is appropriate. The challenge of determining what is appropriate and when can be addressed with the Staircase Model described below.

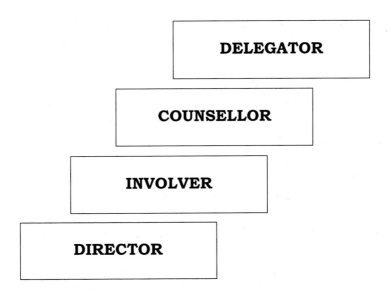

The Staircase Model as developed in the book, *Escape from Oz - Leadership for the 21st Century* describes the four different leadership strategies of how leaders may communicate with staff members who report to them.

The knowledge and skill set of the employee and the task that is being considered determines which stair of the Staircase Model the leader should be standing on with the employee. Think of the strategies as a flight of stairs with the bottom stair being the narrowest. This first stair is called **director**, because there is a lot of direction that comes from the leader to the employee. If the employee is new to the job at hand or has minimum knowledge, they need to be told what to do, how to do it, when, and why. The leader makes the decisions. If a leader leads an employee from the higher stairs of the model which have more autonomy for the employee, this way of leading leaves the employee feeling unsupported.

The second stair is wider because it involves more responsibility, more decision making and a wider frame of reference. A leader who is communicating from stair two is an **involver**. They involve the follower in making the decision by listening to their perspective and ideas and then making the decision.

The third stair is a **counsellor** or coach role and is best used once the employee has the skill set and information to make a decision, but still looks to their leader to help them clarify decisions before they are made. The leader offers support and asks the employee what he thinks and then coaches him to a decision.

It is at this third stair where the decision making shifts from the leader to the employee - where a leader coaches

the employee to a decision, helps the employee to see the missing pieces or plays 'devil's advocate' so the employee can see any cracks in their plan.

The fourth stair is a **delegator** role where the employee has sufficient confidence and competence to carry out the job or task with minimum input or direction.

If a leader leads from the bottom couple of stairs with a highly competent and confident employee, that employee will feel suffocated and micromanaged. If a leader leads from the top couple of stairs with an employee who has little task or organizational understanding, that employee will feel unsupported and see their leader as an abdicator of their role of manager.

Managers have a predominant or preferential way of leading others, a particular stair they wish to stand on. It might be a strategy learned from other managers or leaders who led them in the past. It might have been the first style they latched on to when they entered the work world. Regardless of what their current style might be, they need to question whether it is too inflexible for leading Gen Ys as they go from the **director** stair up to the **delegator** stair. Leaders must be flexible and adapt to the growing competence of the Gen Y employee to ensure that maximum productivity results and that employees feel a high level of job satisfaction.

Gen Ys need to understand (just as when you climb actual stairs) that you are steady and safe when you climb the stairs in order – climbing the first, then the second, then the third and finally the fourth. You take risks with your career safety by jumping over any of the steps to get to the top more quickly.

Leaders often want a simple answer to the leadership question, even though it may not be the most effective. The Staircase Model is based on flexibility and adaptability. Leaders need to be flexible in their strategy and adapt to the needs of the scenario and person they are leading. Focus must not only be on who is being led and their competence and confidence, but on the current situation and the tasks being faced.

Value Alignment and Focused Onboarding

When we consider that Generation Y of all generations is the quickest to move to other opportunities, tools that assist a leader in maximizing their commitment are important. Two areas to consider are value alignment and focused onboarding.

Value Alignment

An employee's knowledge of their organizational values and clarity of their own personal values impact their retention and engagement in their organization. In the *Journal of Business Ethics,* Posner and Schmidt studied the correlation between engagement and personal and organizational values. They found that people who have the clearest understanding about both organizational and their own personal values have the highest level of commitment and engagement.

Here are their findings:

Low clarity on own values + low clarity on organizational values = Commitment Score of 4.90

Low clarity on own values + high clarity on organizational values = Commitment Score of 4.87

High clarity on own values + low clarity on organizational values = Commitment Score of 6.12

High clarity on own values + high clarity on organizational values = Commitment Score of 6.26

Surprisingly, the score was not significantly less for those who have high clarity of personal values, but low clarity on organizational values.

This study raises a couple of interesting observations. It seems that people can be very clear about the organization's values and still not be highly committed to the organization. The people who are clear on who they are but can't recite your mission, vision or values are more likely to stick around and give the 110% than those who wrote the corporate values but are unclear as to who they are as individuals.

How can we use this knowledge as a tool for recruitment, retention and engagement?

1 - Immediately in the recruitment process begin the discussion of values. If the candidate is unsure what values mean, describe situations in your workplace that illustrate your corporate values and test their reactions. The sooner you come to an awareness of the degree of alignment the better. Many hiring decisions are based on experience, education, references, attitude - all great components - but do not forget to include this essential values piece that may determine the success of this individual in your organization.

2 - Challenge the honeymoon phase theory of human resource management. The honeymoon period discussion goes something like this, "He seemed like such a great

candidate - great references, good educational match - but after a few months he seemed to settle back into second gear and stay there."

Every generation has a natural desire to be in a workplace that aligns with their own personal values, but Gen Ys to an even greater degree. This desire is unconscious unless we have spent the time figuring out who we are and what we stand for as individuals. We just know that we don't 'fit' well. When the values in the workplace don't align with our own, soon we break down into a compliant, non-committed level of engagement. Certainly, individuals slip into non-commitment and mere compliance for many reasons – and value misalignment may be the cause. If this is the root of the slide into compliance, you then have a choice of re-selling them on your organization, showing them how what they personally value connects strongly to the organization's values and goals, or letting them go on to other opportunities where they would be more aligned and therefore happier and more productive.

3 - Create learning tools for employees to understand their personal values. Provide opportunities and resources for individual employees to understand who they are - their perspectives, values and beliefs.

The challenge illuminated by this information is for an employer to identify the values that align with job candidates. An ability for an organization to say "This is us!" and for a candidate to be able to say "This is me!" is crucial for the employee's success and engagement in the organization.

Employees who have the greatest clarity about both their personal and your organizational values will have the highest degree of commitment to the organization.

Focused Onboarding

Also known as orientation, the onboarding process in organizations has been reduced from weeks to days by many organizations. Ironically this is not due to the preferences of Gen Y employees who want to hit the ground running, but due to economic reasons. Orientation instructor salaries, facility space rental, not to mention the non-profit-generating time of new employees spent in the training centre, all impact the time that organizations donate to orientation.

Many onboarding processes are equally effective on line as they are in a room with a PowerPoint projector and a flipchart. Once a Gen Y is hired, they want to get moving with their new career opportunity. Question your processes. Often except for belief changing training (such as diversity or leadership), many hours of onboarding time could be put into online opportunities that new Gen Y employees could access anytime and anywhere.

Although Gen Ys prefer shorter orientations, key processes should not be taken lightly. Many Gen Ys need clear goal plans for their careers including mentoring opportunities that are planned in cooperation with their manager or human resource professional. It is important that a Gen Y's career goals and plan be tied to the values of the organization and to their personal goals. A Gen Y

wants to know what the plan is for them in the workplace and how this new job will help their long term career goals.

Be Flexible with Time and Process

Time is money. Or is money time? Members of the three previous generations often valued overtime opportunities for the extra pay offered. Gen Ys however value time off more highly than extra pay. They believe that time is more rewarding than money. Take the example of a Gen Y who continues to live with his or her parents. Without the drive of having to pay a mortgage or other large bills, that Gen Y is highly likely to take their overtime pay as time off instead of as a larger paycheck.

It is important for leaders to empathize with Gen Ys about the value of time off. If a Gen Y staff person wishes time off or to come in later than their usual start time, instead of automatically saying yes or no, a leader can use that opportunity to negotiate a deadline or work load from the Gen Y who wants the time break.

Leaders who are used to seeing only an approve or don't approve option, can take advantage of this flexibility to still get the work done but not necessarily in the way it has been done in the past.

In this chapter we discussed areas where leaders can be more effective when managing Gen Ys. The next chapter will discuss workplace strategies for Gen Ys to succeed.

Chapter Ten

Workplace Strategies for Gen Ys

For Gen Ys, being both a distinct generation and the youngest in the workplace comes with unique challenges. It is not enough for Gen Ys to see themselves as a younger generation from older generations, it is important for Gen Ys to understand how each of the previous generations are different from each other if they are going to maximize their influence.

The following issues are further identified to assist both Gen Ys and their managers in understanding the workplace with the goal of seeing both parties increase their influence and success.

Keep Invisible Relatives out of the Workplace

"Thanks kiddo."

"Oh you remind me of my son."

"That is just what my daughter would have said."

"I didn't think you kids cared about stuff like that."

If you are a Gen Y it is hard to know how to take a comment like those above. Is it a compliment or not? To the youngest generation in the workplace, having their behaviour connected to the age or competence of the relatives of a colleague is both inappropriate and annoying. What has the fact that a Gen Y is the same age as someone's daughter or grandson matter to the workplace? It doesn't really. Although it is human nature to see a behaviour or a trait that reminds you of another person, connecting our workplace and personal relationships can complicate our work reality and muddy up the waters of communication.

Certainly, we will always have moments when one person reminds us in some way of another person. When a Boomer says that her younger colleague reminds her of her nephew, or a Gen Y comments to a Traditionalist that the older employee reminds the Gen Y of her granddad, those relatives come into the conversation. The key to an effective relationship is to keep such comments in our heads and not to verbalize them.

Consider this real life situation:

A Boomer manager has six Gen Y staffers who work for her in a personal medical care service. She found that although there were many great characteristics of her Gen Y staff, she was annoyed by two behaviours: they didn't clean up after themselves in the coffee room and they often wanted cash advances. Those that requested the cash advances usually did not pay the advance back on time, leaving her to contort the payroll documentation to make it all work out and balance.

On the surface it looked like she had a staff problem, but as we dug under the obvious, we saw that she was as much at cause as those whom she managed.

We found that she communicated with her staff using comments such as:

"Hey kids!"

"Do I have to clean up after you like I am your mother?"

"If you run low before payday I can help you out."

Although she didn't compare specific members of her staff to her children, the message got through that she would backfill their negative behaviour. If they didn't clean up their mess, she would. If they burned through their paycheque, she would make sure that they had cash flow. Exactly as a parent would do.

A Traditionalist, Boomer and even a Gen X would say it is only common sense that a person would clean up after themselves and budget their pay. But common sense is influenced by other factors and this manager created an environment that mimicked the child-parent relationship.

Once her behaviour and its impact were brought to her attention, she slowly changed her expectations of her staff and how she communicated that information through feedback to them. The end result was an improvement in their accountability while at the same time creating a more professional relationship on all sides.

Understand Your Digital Privilege

Traditionalists learned the technology of their generation as children and youth. Baby Boomers learned the technology of their generation in their childhood and youth. Traditionalists learned the technology of the succeeding Boomer generation as *adults*.

Gen Xs learned the technology of their generation as children and youth. Traditionalists and Baby Boomers learned the technology of the Gen X generation as adults.

Gen Y is learning the technology of their generation as children and youth. Traditionalists, Baby Boomers and Gen Xs are learning the technology of the Gen Y generation as adults.

In the generation following Generation Y, probably to be called Generation Z, the Traditionalists, Baby Boomers, Gen Xs and Gen Ys will all be learning the technology of the Gen Z generation as adults.

In our growing up years, we all had the luxury of learning the latest technology. As our generation ages, we need to learn the technology of the newest generation. When we say that older workers have difficulty learning new technology, we are looking at the situation upside down. Traditionalists have had to learn the most new technology of all four generations.

Every generation has taught the preceeding generations the latest technologies. Traditionalists familiar with ping pong were taught Pong by Boomers. Boomers were taught Nintendo by Gen X. Gen Y is teaching everyone about Wii. Gen Z will teach Gen Ys whatever technology will be next.

Privacy

Traditionalists say "come on over", Boomers say "give me a call before you come by", Gen Xs say "email me and we will schedule something" and Gen Ys say "text me before you call". Ironically, each new generation has become more closed when it comes to physical privacy. At the same time, each new generation is less closed when it comes to privacy on-line.

Traditionalists, Boomers and Gen Xs are cautious about their social networking footprint. Gen Ys however are less cautious and may post ideas, pictures or links that may reflect negatively on them in the workplace. Certainly there is an argument to be made that what is on Facebook has no connection to the work a person does, however all employees must consider that managers and human resource professionals are looking to understand the 'whole you' before they hire you. Secondly if you represent your organization in any way to the public, your personal

life becomes your professional life. Like the employee who wears a shirt with his organization's logo on the front and gets drunk at the football game, today's seamless digital world has created new and annoying realities.

Career Paths and Organizational Reality

When we think of career paths, we most often think about getting a job and moving up to more well paid and responsible positions. This career path is neither desirable nor obtainable for us all. Let's look at the four types of career paths and the types of organizations that match each path.

Researchers D. Foot, R. Venne and M.J. Driver describe the four paths as: steady, linear, spiral and transitory.

The 'steady' path, according to Venne, defines a career as "a vocation or calling, basically a lifelong commitment to a field with little actual job movement". It can be a professional or trades oriented career (doctor, journeyperson electrician, teacher, minister of a religious group) where you have one profession and often one employer for your entire career. The benefits of this type of career path are one of fringe benefits and longevity. These benefits may be often obtained through collective bargaining or set salary rates for the profession.

The 'linear' career path is the one we are most familiar with and the one that society suggests is desired by us all. Unlike the 'steady' career path, this path is one of upward mobility where we work in only a couple of occupations and for one or two organizations. To achieve

this career path, the organization must be shaped like a pyramid with a large lower base narrowing into a high upper point. Employees enter en masse and 'climb the ladder' to more and more success. The shape of the organization that allows for such a career path must be a narrow triangle and growing. If the organization is not on a high growth pattern and taking in new employees to expand the base, it becomes a flattened pyramid and the 'linear' career path becomes less guaranteed. Successful entrepreneurial endeavours where a person joins the organization at its inception guarantee a linear path as the organization grows and expands, but organizations in slow growth or regression will flatten.

The third path is the 'spiral' path that we find ourselves on when we work in a flattened pyramid. We think we want upward mobility however there are too many of us and too few opportunities for promotion. We move slowly up and then over and around, slowly up and then over and around – spiralling upward a bit at a time. We trade in our goals of authority for education, retraining and experiences. We may have multiple types of jobs within one organization. The organization promotes lifelong learning and may even create titles such as Manager for non-managerial roles to engage a workforce that they cannot promote. Many organizations in Canada today have this structure and limited career path options for upward mobility.

The last career path described by Driver and Venne is one that is 'transitory' where a person would have multiple employers and multiple jobs over their lifetime. The person jumps from lily pad to lily pad, as they work on

temporary teams and projects. Those involved in creative endeavours (film makers, actors) or short term work (contractors and consultants) would move laterally for opportunities, which may or may not be upwardly mobile.

As we are all too well aware in our current economy, the fast race to the top of the organization is a myth and has been for some time, as Baby Boomers and Gen Xs in some large organizations or government agencies can attest.

For a Gen Y just starting on their career path there is no time like the present to decide what career path he or she wishes to have and what types of organizations or employment opportunities would best match his or her goals.

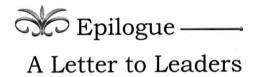 Epilogue ————

A Letter to Leaders

Canada is facing a labour challenge and the race for employees will be won by those organizations that recognize their demographic challenges and address them before it is too late. C. Handy wrote in the journal *Leader to Leader* that organizations have 'sigmoid curves' where the normal life cycle is one of "steady growth that inevitably one day peaks and turns into decline".

Our traditional workforce is in the declining portion of a sigmoid curve. The challenge is to ensure the security of our organizations by starting to construct a second curve before the decline of the previous one is complete. The race for employees will be won by organizations that begin their new curves early and manage the corresponding fall out of the old curve, including the resistance to change that occurs when management and employees perceive that they are still succeeding with old processes and systems.

Canada's low birth rates combined with the retirement of the youngest part of the Traditionalist generation and the oldest part of the Baby Boomer generation has many organizations worried about labour shortages. Even with Canada's economic conditions generally slowing, labour shortages in certain geographic areas and specific skill sets are still in crisis.

While some organizations stay on their declining curves as they continue to merely study the situation, organizations who have jumped to their next curve are taking action. As well as aggressively pursuing Gen Y employees, they have also set their sights on recruitment with groups that have historically been under-represented in the workforce (Aboriginal persons, women in non-traditional or management roles, persons with disabilities and persons of visible minority). This pursuit involves changing recruiting, retention and leadership strategies to ensure new employees stay and become fully committed to the organization.

These changes unfortunately also have the potential to create upheaval in current systems and trigger fear and resistance amongst existing employees. The role of the leader, therefore, is to mitigate the fear and resistance from those in the existing system while attracting and retaining a new workforce.

Fear and Resistance to Diversity

Fear and resistance to a diverse workforce are rooted in an employee's concern about how the change will affect them personally. Will they need to communicate differently? Behave differently? Will the culture change

enough to make them uncomfortable? Will they still feel like they fit in and belong? These questions must be addressed or the workplace may become ineffective and unproductive.

J.P Kotter, writing in the *Harvard Business Review*, suggests that leadership is more important in times of change and crisis. To attract new staff and hold on to existing employees requires the ability to both motivate and inspire thus satisfying the basic human needs of employees including their feelings of having control over their lives. Unfortunately when change is happening around people, they do not feel 'in control' of their lives. This is especially so when they did not initiate the change involved.

Creating a diverse workforce to win the employee race often means a shift of workplace norms. It also requires people to think and communicate with others differently. These changes can be painful and emotional for many employees.

A manager's reaction is a vital key to creating a respectful workplace as his team becomes more diverse. When reacting to change-based resistance, a leader can fuse with his staff, disconnect from his staff, or differentiate himself from his staff and their emotions.

Fusion occurs when the leader cannot separate himself or herself emotionally from those he or she leads, allowing his or her own emotions to be merely reactions to what others say and do. The distress of the staff triggers anxiety for the leader, and the leader then allows his or her own anxiety to control the situation.

The leader may demand that others express only positive thoughts and feelings about the change, a behaviour that creates an outcome where the leader does not know what is occurring as employees know not to tell 'the whole truth'.

Ultimately, under fusion, the leader can give in to the demands caused by the staff's distress thus sacrificing his or her own vision or goal.

Disconnection is too much separation between the leader and the emotions of his employees, where the disconnected leader has no sense of how his subordinates are feeling or what they think about the changes. He might even perceive responding to the emotions of others as unprofessional. The leader takes into consideration only his or her own workplace goals, ignoring the emotional turmoil of his or her team members, and creating an environment of rumour and dissention.

With fear of diversity in the workplace, the leader must notice that his team members are upset with the change, but not react to it. This **self-differentiation** occurs when a leader is both connected to and separate from his employees, clear about performance expectations, true to his or her own vision, while listening and seeking to understand the fears and objections of the people on the team.

My role when consulting to clients is often to design and deliver training to the existing staff that explores the emotions they are feeling and addresses stereotypes that fuel negative communication. To initiate and implement workplace changes where the employees come from diverse backgrounds or talents requires a leader to have

a clear understanding of how his or her emotions come into play in the process and to be able to balance the need to support his or her staff while advancing his or her objective.

When a large number of diverse people (such as from one racial or generational group) enter a workplace, the potential for loss of culture must be managed by the leader. We need workplace cultures to give meaning to our lives at work and so we need to define and learn acceptable rules of workplace behaviour. This is why we must discuss ethics at work (or work ethics).

No one is immune to how diversity impacts corporate culture. The new people coming in lose something, the people in the existing system lose something, and still both sides feel that they are not truly represented in the new system. The changing culture must take in the concerns of those in the system, those entering it and the organization itself.

Attracting and Retaining a Diverse Workforce

The focus of my consultancy work is to assist managers in understanding diversity issues so they can attract, retain and engage the workforce they wish. Diversity can mean the large ways we see ourselves as different (such as gender, race, generations and disability) or the smaller ways that can also create workplace conflict (such as values, mental processing or family systems).

My efforts are not only about helping managers understand diversity, but also about assisting them to develop appropriate thoughts and skills when working with people

who they see as being different from themselves. This requires courage to learn new ways of behaving plus self-discipline to continue learning and practicing new ways of communicating instead of using what is the most comfortable - even if it is the least effective.

Seeing the world as others see it is a challenge. To do this effectively, leaders must understand the complexity of diversity without being drawn into new stereotypes, be holistic in their approach to strategy and take a political view of all employees' needs.

Balancing Respect for Existing Employees While Recruiting New

It is important to balance our fast pace in the race for new employees with cool-headed thoughts about the long term impact of our strategies. Without understanding the impact of initiatives designed to attract one generational group, a leader can create long term damage in relationships with other generations.

Consider the case of CN RAIL. In 2007, CEO Hunter Harrison was quoted in *The Globe and Mail* saying "CN's labour strife can be traced to a clash between a pension focused, aging workforce and management's desire to recruit young employees willing to tackle flexible hours and work weekends". This quote was followed shortly by news that the United Transportation Union planned to file a discrimination complaint against CN.

In an effort to increase younger workers in its organization, CN did not look at the impact of their internal and external messages on the generational

groups in their workforce. The attempt to recruit new staff was seen to be at the expense of respect for existing members.

Conclusion

Effective change of workplace demographics is not accidental. To have the best people in a diverse workplace, organizations must identify their diversity issues, pursue new employee groups, manage the fallout with existing employees and create new cultural norms that both respect the future and honour the past.

 Notes and References ──────

Notes

Generation refers to the generational group. **Gen** as in Gen X or Gen Y refers to individuals of that group.

Where the term **he** or **she** or other gender pronouns are used, consider the gender interchangeable with the other.

References: Chapter One

1. Mathews, T.J., Hamilton, B.E. (2009) *Delayed childbearing: More women are having their first child later in life.* NCHS data brief, no 21. Hyattsville, MD: National Center for Health Statistics.

2. Wohl, Robert (1979). *The generation of 1914.* Cambridge, Mass.: Harvard University Press. pp. 203–209.

3. Comte, Auguste, *Cours de Philosophie Positive* (The Course in Positivist Philosophy) was a series of texts written between 1830 and 1842. The works were translated into English by Harriet Martineau and condensed to form: *The Positive Philosophy of Auguste Comte;* 2 volumes; Chapman, 1853 (reissued by Cambridge University Press, 2009; ISBN 978-1-108-00118-2).

4. Pilcher, Jane (September 1994). Mannheim's Sociology of Generations: An undervalued legacy. *British Journal of Sociology* 45 (3): 481–495.

5. Howe, N., & Strauss, W. (2007), *The next 20 years: How customer and workforce attitudes will evolve.* Harvard Business Review *85*(7), 41–52.

6. Foot, David K. (1996). *Boom Bust & Echo.* Toronto: Macfarlane Walter & Ross.

7. Tapscott, D. (2009). *Grown up digital: How the net generation is changing your world.* New York: McGraw-Hill.

8. Zemke, R., Raines, C. and Filipczak, B. (2000). *Generations at work: Managing the clash of veterans, boomers, Xers, and nexters in your workplace.* New York: AMACOM American Management Association.

9. Tulgan, B. (2009). *Not everyone gets a trophy.* San Francisco: Jossey-Bass.

10. The Washington Post, *Some Call it Jones.* April 6, 2000.

References: **Chapter Three**

1. Fong, Francis. *Older Workers Stampede into the Labour Market:* Observations TD Economics, February 23, 2012, www.td.com.economics.

2. Sladek, Sarah (2011). *The End of Membership as we Know It.* Washington, DC: ASAE.

References: **Chapter Four**

1. Foot, David K. (1996). *Boom Bust & Echo.* Toronto: Macfarlane Walter & Ross.

References: **Chapter Six**

1. *The Regina Leader Post,* "Edmonton Teacher who fought 'no-zero' policy is fired" Sept 15, 2012.

2. *The Regina Leader Post,* "Teacher who handed out zeros expects to be fired" June 2, 2012.

3. Edmonton School Board website - www.Epsd.ca.

References: **Chapter Eight**

1. Gibson, J.W., Greenwood, R.A. and Murphy, Jr, E.F. (2009) Generational Differences in the Workplace: Personal Values, Behaviors and Popular Beliefs. *Journal of Diversity Management,* 4(3).

References: Chapter Nine

1. Gallos, J., Editor (2008). *Business leadership*, Second Edition. San Francisco, CA: Jossey Bass.

2. Martinson, J. (2000) *Escape from Oz - Leadership for the 21st Century*. Regina, SK: Martrain

3. Kouzes, J. & Posner, B. (2007). *A leadership challenge*. San Francisco, CA: John Wiley & Sons

References: Chapter Ten

1. Venne, R (2011). Mentoring: Bridging the Generational and Career Divide, *Adapting Mentorship Across the Professions*, pp. 107-122, Calgary, Alberta: Temeron books.

2. Venne, R. (2010). Longer to launch: Demographic changes in life-course transitions, *Ways of Living: Work, Community and Lifestyle Choices*. New York: Palgrave Macmillan, pp75-98.

References: Epilogue

1. Handy, C. (2002). Elephants and fleas: is your organization prepared for change? *Leader to Leader, 24* (Spring) 29–33.

2. Kotter, J.P. (2001). What leaders really do. *Harvard Business Review, 79* (11) 85 – 96.

3. CN Boss Bemoans Workforce Rules (2007, April 12). *The Globe and Mail*, p. B1.

4. CN Union Planning to File Discrimination Complaint (2007, April 13). *The Globe and Mail*, p. B1.

 Index ———

 Acknowledgements

Thanks first to the many clients and workshop participants that have shared their ideas, perspectives and challenges around generational issues with me.

Secondly, I would like to thank my reader team (Carol Stepenoff, Carolyn Schur, Malcolm Bucholtz, Laurelie Martinson, Pat Dell, Kathleen Thompson, Cindy Hauck, Nancy Bowey, Pamela Burns and Colleen Smith) for their great feedback and insights.

Lastly, I would like to thank you, my reader, for picking up this book and spending time with these ideas. I hope you find this book pithy and practical.

Jeanne Martinson

〰 Author Biography ────

Jeanne Martinson, M.A., is a professional speaker, trainer and best-selling author who has worked internationally and throughout Canada. Since co-founding her own firm, MARTRAIN Corporate and Personal Development in 1993, Jeanne has inspired thousands of participants in her workshops and keynote presentations with her humour, insight and real-world examples.

Jeanne became interested in training while working for a Fortune 500 company in southern California. Back in her home province of Saskatchewan, she side-stepped into sales and marketing for ten years - where in the printing and labelling industry, she took a $25,000 sales territory and grew it to $850,000 within four years.

Jeanne recently completed her Master of Arts degree in Leadership at Royal Roads University in Victoria, British Columbia, Canada. Her graduate research focused on the

differences and similarities of criminal gang leaders and corporate leaders. Her research was published by the International Leadership Association in their annual journal (2012) as a peer-reviewed journal article (Leadership Lessons from the Criminal World). See information on the journal in the following pages.

Jeanne also holds a Certificate in Organisational (Organizational) Behaviour from Heriot-Watt University (Edinburgh, Scotland) and is certified as a practitioner of NLP (Neuro Linguistic Programming).

As Managing Partner of her own firm, Jeanne delivers workshops and keynote addresses to government, associations and the private sector. Her most popular topics are leadership and diversity. As a Canadian best-selling author and strategist in workplace diversity, Jeanne's goal is to assist leaders in understanding diversity issues so they may attract, retain and engage their ideal workforce.

In July 1999, Jeanne released her first non-fiction book titled *Lies and Fairy Tales That Deny Women Happiness* which explores the myths that many Canadian women are raised with and which limit their ability to have happy relationships and fulfilling careers.

Her second book, *Escape from Oz - Leadership For The 21st Century* was released in October 2001. This book explores the parallels of the characters in the fable *The Wonderful Wizard of Oz* and our own beliefs about personal and professional leadership.

Jeanne's third book, *War & Peace in the Workplace - Diversity, Conflict, Understanding, Reconciliation* was released September 2005. This book explores how

workplaces are becoming more diverse and how diversity may trigger conflict. The book illustrates how we have the choice of allowing conflict to spiral down into dysfunction or of taking charge, becoming aware and developing understanding.

Jeanne takes a leading role in her community, a dedication that was recognized with the awarding of the Canada 125 Medal, the YWCA Women of Distinction Award in the category of Business, Labor and Professions, the Centennial Leadership Award for outstanding contribution to the Province of Saskatchewan, the Athena Award, and the national Diversity award – the EMCY.

Jeanne has been listed in Who's Who of Canadian Women since 1996 and Canadian Who's Who since 1999. Jeanne is Past President of: Saskatchewan Training and Development Association (Regina Chapter), Saskatchewan Business and Professional Women, and Women Entrepreneurs of Saskatchewan. She was Founding President of the Saskatchewan Chapter of the Canadian Association of Professional Speakers (CAPS).

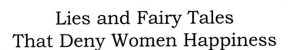

Lies and Fairy Tales
That Deny Women Happiness

In July 1999, Jeanne released her first nonfiction book which explores the myths that many Canadian women are raised with and which limit their ability to have happy relationships and fulfilling careers.

As women, we have grown up to believe in stories that impact our abilities, desires, roles and potential. Some of these stories are presented as 'fairy tales'. These myths we hear as small children influence our perspectives and help determine whether we see ourselves as victims or self-determined women.

This book is available in print, as an audio book and as an Ebook. See www.wooddragonbooks.com.

Escape from Oz – Leadership for the 21st Century

This book explores the parallels of the characters in the fable *The Wonderful Wizard of Oz* and our own beliefs about personal and professional leadership.

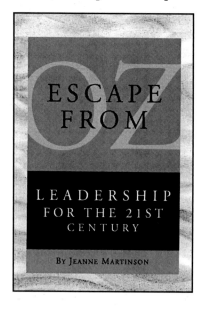

The first part of the book explores the four cornerstones required to be effective leaders: insight, courage, self-discipline and influence over others. The second part of the book explores how we can move out of our comfort zone to lead individuals according to their reality, skill set and knowledge base - with the goal of achieving trust and long term success.

This book about the basics of personal leadership and leading others is written to assist you in becoming an effective leader – whether you are leading a committee of five or a corporation of five thousand.

This book is available in print, as an audio book and as an Ebook. See www.wooddragonbooks.com.

War and Peace in the Workplace –
Diversity, Conflict, Understanding, Reconciliation

Ever wonder why we can't just get along? Why we react to each other the way we do?

Most conflict in the workplace comes from our differences - both our diversity in the big 'D' issues such as race, gender or ability but also diversity in the small 'd' issues such as values, marital and family status, age or thought processes.

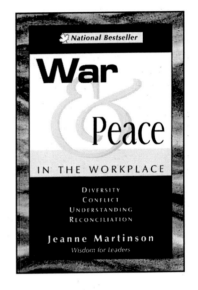

Diversity can be problematic and it can be wonderful. As individuals and organizations, we can benefit from the many perspectives that create the synergy to move an organization forward by leaps and bounds. On the other hand, differences can bring conflict, toxic work groups, low morale, harassment, misunderstandings and employee turnover.

Many organizations adopt respectful workplace or harassment policies. But this isn't enough to realize the benefits of a diverse workforce or to minimize diversity-based conflict. We need to shift how we perceive and work with others. This book illustrates how we have the choice of allowing conflict to spiral down into dysfunction or of taking charge, becoming aware and developing understanding. It's all up to you!

This book is available in print, as an audio book and as an Ebook. See www.wooddragonbooks.com.

Leading in Complex Worlds

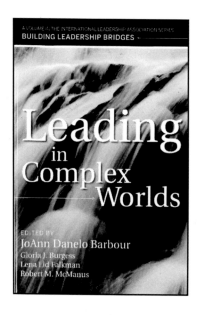

Leading in Complex Worlds was released June 2012 by publisher Jossey-Bass. This collection of chapters from leadership experts and scholars is the annual peer-reviewed journal of the International Leadership Association. It contains chapters from fifteen authors, including a chapter by Jeanne Martinson titled ***Leadership Lessons from the Criminal World*** which is based on her Master of Arts graduate degree research that compared criminal and corporate leaders.

Other chapters are:
* Leadership Education: The Power of Storytelling
* Black Women's Political Leadership Development: Recentering the Leadership Discourse
* Soccer Tactics and Complexity Leadership
* The Role of Culture and History in the Applicability of Western Leadership Theories in Africa
* A Tao Complexity Tool, Leading from Being
* The Leadership of Dr. Jane Goodall: A Four Quadrant Perspective

This book is available in print.
See www.wooddragonbooks.com.

Leadership and Diversity
Keynote Presentations
available with Jeanne Martinson

Looking for a speaker for a staff development day, conference or convention?

Leadership for the 21st Century

In the fable, "The Wonderful Wizard of Oz", the Lion, Scarecrow and Tin Man desired courage, a brain and a heart. They believed the only path to achieving their desires was the Wizard's magic. Humans often wish for 'leadership skills'. Like the Oz characters, we have everything we need to succeed. We don't need a magic pill to be successful leaders - only a willingness to recognize our potential and develop it!

Leadership Communication That Gets Results

It is human nature to fall into our most comfortable way of communicating as a leader - regardless of whether that style is giving us the results we want or not! By learning how to lead individuals according to the situation, their competency and commitment, we can utilize our employees' abilities to the maximum!

Generations in the Workplace: Making Peace Between Gen Xs and Boomers

For the first time, there are four generations in the workplace. Traditionalists, Boomers, Gen Xs and Gen Ys all have different values and goals. And those values and goals are creating conflict!

War and Peace in the Workplace: Diversity, Conflict, Understanding, Reconciliation

Ever wonder why we just can't get along? Individual differences - large and small - often create conflict between people. We have the choice of allowing conflict to spiral down into dysfunction or of taking action, becoming aware and developing understanding. It's all up to us.

Nurture, Nature or Just Nasty? Understanding Male and Female Leadership Styles

When women lead like men, they are called nasty names, when men are encouraged to lead like women, they are wimps. How are we different? How can we use our differences to be great leaders?

Leadership and Diversity Workshops
with Jeanne Martinson

Understanding Diversity in Today's Workplace

Respect in the workplace comes from the foundational understanding that we are different from everyone else. Sometimes these differences are the big 'D' differences such as race, gender or disability. Sometimes the differences that create judgment and conflict arise from small 'd' differences - how we see the world, whether we feel our values have been compromised or ignored, how we see the work should be done, even how we think our colleagues should behave.

This workshop explores:
- what is diversity to us as individuals and how is it defined according to human rights codes and labour law
- how we develop our beliefs and how those beliefs affect how we see colleagues, the work that needs to be done, and how it should be completed
- how our mind naturally creates generalizations and stereotypes
- how we interpret our common values and how they play out in our everyday behaviours to possibly create conflict
- how we and others change as we become aware of diversity
- how our environment supports some groups while creates barriers for others
- vital information about key areas of diversity in our workplace such as: generations, gender and gender

identity, left brain/right brain differences, Aboriginal/non Aboriginal differences, religion, visible minority issues and physical and intellectual disabilities

- how people react to diversity
- what emotions do employees experience as their workforce becomes more diverse and challenges occur
- what can a diverse workforce offer an organization
- the consequences to ourselves, the organization and our colleagues of communicating based only on our perspective
- how we read into a situation what is happening and create judgments based on our interpretation of other people's intentions
- strategies to move from diversity based conflict to understanding and reconciliation.

Managing and Working with a Multi-Generational Workforce

For the first time, there are four generations in the workplace. Traditionalists, Boomers, Gen Xs and Gen Ys all have different values and goals. And those values and goals can create conflict.

Overview

- What understanding generational diversity gives an organization
- How generational information relates to overall diversity in the workplace
- The four generational groupings
- Impact of cusp years
- Caveats (exceptions) to generational data
- Why demographers disagree as to when generational groupings begin and end
- How the current economic downturn impacts our managing of the generations.

Traditionalists/Baby Boomers/Gen X/Gen Y

- Other terms for each generation
- Born in what years
- Influences in childhood and early adulthood that shaped their perspective
- Behaviours demonstrated due to those influences

Beliefs in the workplace of the four generations regarding

- Authority
- Hierarchy
- Loyalty
- Job Security

- Change
- Job Change
- Activity and productivity
- Structure
- Work Flow
- Communication
- Information
- Time
- Power
- Flexibility

Ways to address clash of generational communication

Organizational issues regarding the four generational groups

- How to attract the four generations
- How to retain the four generations
- How to engage/motivate the four generations

Leading A Diverse Workforce

The ability to lead a diverse workforce has become one of the most important skills in the workplace today. This program is designed to assist leaders in understanding diversity and leadership issues so they may attract, retain and engage their ideal workforce.

Segment One: Cornerstones of Leadership

In this segment participants learn about the four cornerstones of leadership, the differences between leadership and management and how to build and maintain trust.

- Leaders and Managers
- The Four Cornerstones of Leadership
- Influence and Trust

Segment Two: Our Leadership Thoughts and Behaviours

It is important that we understand how it is that we think, how we interpret others behaviour and how they interpret our behaviour as leaders. It is vital for leaders to understand how their thoughts drive their communication choices and processes.

- How We Think and Communicate With Ourselves
- Exceptional Feedback Models

Segment Three: Diversity Skilled Leaders

It is essential that leaders understand the diversity that exists in their team, their stakeholder group and the clients they serve. This segment covers vital information regarding each of the diversity areas found in today's workplace.

Segment Four: Growing Your Team

The leaders in your organization must know how to bring about the best in the people they work with. It is essential that leaders be trustworthy and encourage employees to grow and excel to the best of their abilities. This requires understanding how to influence team members to continue doing what is needed and to change behaviours and attitudes that hold back the success of the team and organization.

This segment includes performance models to assist in the uncovering and solving of core problems, the 'four stairs to leadership' communication and delegation model and conflict models of how we and others respond to challenges.

- Team - What Does It Look Like
- The Staircase to Delegating to Others
- Conflict Modes Leadership Perspective
- Six Hats Problems Solving
- Performance Management Tool

To contact Jeanne Martinson

to discuss working with your organization

See: www.martrain.org

or call

306.569.0388